Cancer As An Opportunity
Transforming Pessimism Into Optimism

By

Thomas A. Myers

The information contained in Cancer as an Opportunity™ is not intended as a substitute for the advice of a physician or other qualified mental health professional. Readers who suspect they may have specific mental health problems should consult a physician or other qualified mental health professional about any suggestions made.

Copyright © 2016 by Thomas A. Myers

All Rights Reserved

ISBN: 978-0-9986079-0-0

T. A. Myers & Co.

No part of Cancer as an Opportunity may be reproduced or transmitted in any form or by any means electronic, mechanical, photocopying, recording or otherwise, without the prior written permission of Thomas A. Myers, T. A. Myers & Co., Aspen Business Park 5400 Ward Rd., Building 3, Suite L-40, Arvada, Colorado 80002.

Cover Photograph: Author, Thomas A. Myers, surfing on Oahu's North Shore, circa 1980.

What Top Cancer-Care Experts Have Said About *Cancer As An Opportunity:*

Anne Jadwin -- VP of Nursing/Chief Nursing Officer at the award-winning Fox Chase Cancer Center, cited by the U.S. News & World Report as one of the top-ranked, elite hospitals in the country, devoted entirely to cancer care:

> "Your book was inspirational and a pleasure to review. Thanks for the opportunity! I thoroughly enjoyed the format and content of the book and thought it was exceptionally done!"

> "Highest rating, 5 out of 5"

> "I like that your personal stories are shared, and the compelling text holds the readers interest."

> "The self-recorded visualization exercises to reprogram the anxiety response have tremendous potential to help our cancer patients."

> "One of the things I liked best was the evidence-based approach and the book's overall positive tone."

Laura Beaupre -- Manager, Oncology Navigation Team, Cancer Support Services for the Lehigh Valley Health Network, which has achieved national recognition continuously since 1995 as one of the U.S. News & World Report's Best Hospitals:

> "*I love the tool that this book provides.* As a Nurse Navigator, I work closely with hundreds of oncology patients each year, and we discuss the anxiety and depression that comes from feeling a lack of control after a cancer diagnosis. My teaching has always been to control those things that are possible- maintaining healthy diet, staying as active as possible, doing something enjoyable each day. *However, this book takes it to the next level- teaching a way to train the brain to seek positivity and use it to enhance life both during treatment, and after. Anyone -- those affected by cancer and those not -- can benefit from these techniques.*"

> "The fact that Tom writes the book as a cancer survivor, and, as someone who incorporates the principles into his daily life, gives the book credibility. Most books that I have read on the subject of

"coping" with a cancer diagnosis are written in more of a clinical sense from health care professionals. I like that Tom was able to give personal experiences to illustrate his points. I especially liked the reference to his father's experience -- what a great lesson he taught Tom and those around him."

Bridget Bertrand -- oncological nurse, St. Clair, Michigan:

"*Cancer as an Opportunity* is very well organized and well thought out. I can see this book being beneficial to not only adult cancer patients and families, but also families of our pediatric cancer patients. I foresee your book being a huge success and look forward to seeing it on the shelves of bookstores. I will for sure be buying a copy and telling all our oncology families about it. I would definitely recommend this book to families going through cancer treatment. A great resource! Five stars (out of five)."

What Other Cancer Care Specialists Have Said about *Cancer As An Opportunity*:

- ❖ "I liked the personal stories illustrating the points, especially when they came directly from the heart."

- ❖ "I liked the explanation of why the protocol techniques are so effective -- the explanations were well put, in simply explained science."

- ❖ "I liked the protocol techniques, themselves. I will use them, not specifically for cancer in my case, and I will share them."

- ❖ "I really, really liked that you broke down the *rationale* of why each part of the guided visualizations were included. Great! I have not seen this done before."

- ❖ "I like that your emphasis on how even patient prognosis is beside the point -- the point is that we all die so how can we take our life back from what is happening to it -- to enjoy what we've been given? Lovely."

- "The many quotations were well placed and relevant."

- "Honestly, what I liked best about the book was that I hadn't previously heard this profound message -- stated the way you described -- and I immediately wanted to use the tools in my own life. Thank you! 5 stars out of 5!"

- "Good solid science, thank you ☺!"

- "The concepts were very well presented -- using simply explained science -- and offered a practical array of well explained self-help tools. Your life's story is also a special sauce component."

- "I am not a cancer patient/survivor but I am a survivor of a bunch of other things (and have come a long way on turning that straw into gold), and immediately saw how what you're sharing is relevant to more than just cancer. Thank you."

- "I appreciate that cancer patients/loved ones have a focused book written for them. It's needed."

Contents

PART ONE 1

INTRODUCTION 1

    Words from My Father 2

ABOUT THIS BOOK 5

    How to Use This Book 12
    How You Can Apply the "Cancer as an Opportunity" Protocol 14
    A Surfing Lesson 20

CHAPTER ONE: FEAR OF CANCER 28

    The Anatomy of Worry 35

CHAPTER TWO: THE AUTHOR - WHO IS THIS GUY? 37

    My Doghouse Epiphany 46
    The Odyssey Begins 52

PART TWO: WORRY, ANXIETY, AND STRESS 62

CHAPTER THREE: OVERVIEW OF THE CAO PROGRAM 62

CHAPTER FOUR: NEUROSCIENTIFIC FOUNDATION 75

    The Reptilian Brain 78
    The Limbic Brain 79
    The Neocortex 80

CHAPTER FIVE: POSITIVE GUIDED VISUALIZATION 86

    Use of Nurturing Positive Imagery 87
    Brain Conflict and Integration 91
    Rational Thinking, Emotional Imagery, and Body Felt Sensations 96

CHAPTER SIX: THE CAO TREATMENT PROTOCOL 101

    Phase 1: Distinguish Between Destructive and Constructive Worry ... 104
    Phase 2: Contending with Destructive Worry, Anxiety and Stress 106
    Phase 3: Relaxation/Mindfulness Meditation 108
    Phase 4: Positive Reflection (Reverie) 109
    Phase 5: Optimistic Future Visualization 112

PART THREE: PERSONAL IMPLEMENTATION OF PROGRAM 124

CHAPTER SEVEN: LET'S GET STARTED 124

    Deep Breathing 129
    Muscle Relaxation 130
    Peaceful Visualization 131

CHAPTER EIGHT: RELAXING AND FINDING A SAFE PLACE 132

    PROTOCOL SCRIPT 1 - TEXT WITH EXPLANATION 136
    CONCLUDING COMMENTS REGARDING THIS SCRIPT 142

CHAPTER NINE: EXPLORING BODY FELT SENSATIONS 143
    THE NATURE OF BODILY FELT PAIN 144

CHAPTER TEN: MAKING FRIENDS WITH YOUR FEAR 152
    PROTOCOL SCRIPT 2 – TEXT WITH EXPLANATION: 155

CHAPTER ELEVEN: A FEW WORDS ABOUT GUIDED IMAGERY 162

CHAPTER TWELVE: POSITIVE REFLECTION (REVERIE) 165
    ABOUT THIS EXERCISE 165
    PROTOCOL SCRIPT FOR PHASE 3 – TEXT WITH EXPLANATION 168
    ADDITIONAL COMMENTS REGARDING THIS SCRIPT 173

CHAPTER THIRTEEN: OPTIMISTIC FUTURE VISUALIZATION 174
    PROTOCOL SCRIPT 4 – TEXT WITH EXPLANATION 179
    CLOSING COMMENTS ON THIS PROTOCOL SCRIPT 184

CHAPTER FOURTEEN: KICKING IT UP A NOTCH 187
    SHARPEN YOUR SENSORY PERCEPTIONS 188
    SHARE YOUR GOOD FEELINGS WITH OTHERS 189
    PRACTICE LIVING ONE DAY AT A TIME -- MAKE EACH DAY THE BEST! 190
    CONGRATULATE YOURSELF! 190
    COUNT YOUR BLESSINGS AND GIVE THANKS 191
    FURTHER THOUGHTS 192

CHAPTER FIFTEEN: INCREASING CONFIDENCE 194
    PROTOCOL SCRIPT FIVE – TEXT WITH EXPLANATION 195
    BOTTOM LINE 204

EPILOGUE 207

REFERENCES 1

APPENDIX A: PROTOCOL SCRIPTS 1 THROUGH 5 16
    PROTOCOL SCRIPT 1: "RELAXING AND FINDING A SAFE PLACE" 17
    PROTOCOL SCRIPT 2: "RELAXATION AND MAKING FRIENDS WITH YOUR FEAR" ... 22
    PROTOCOL SCRIPT 3: "POSITIVE REFLECTION (REVERIE)" 26
    PROTOCOL SCRIPT 4: "OPTIMISTIC FUTURE VISUALIZATION" 31
    PROTOCOL SCRIPT 5: "INCREASING CONFIDENCE – KICKING IT UP A NOTCH 36

APPENDIX B: MAKING YOUR OWN SCRIPT RECORDINGS 45

APPENDIX C: CONTACT INFORMATION 48

PART ONE
INTRODUCTION

> *"We are meant to discover that we are powerful creators, if not of our entire reality, at least of our experience of reality. We aren't responsible for what each moment holds, but we are responsible for our experience of each moment, because we have the power to make any moment heaven or hell."*
>
> -Gina Lake: *What about Now?*

Former tennis great, Arthur Ashe, once said: "Fear should not be an excuse to come to a standstill. It provides the impetus to step up and strike." Cancer as an Opportunity is a guide to overcoming the fear and dread of cancer. Cancer can be a wake-up call to reorder priorities and commitments that can vastly facilitate emotional and physical wellness. I will discuss the latest techniques, taken from cutting-edge neuroscience and cognitive behavioral psychology to help you with your cancer challenge. I will also discuss why our quest should not be so much for miraculous healing, as for mindfulness -- the greater appreciation of each delicious moment we are on the planet. Our discussion will be up front and personal; this book is addressed to readers who have all, at one time or another, stared into the abyss of a cancer diagnosis and had occasion to ruminate over the apparent grave implications; and to those spouses, caretakers and loved ones who care about how they feel. To begin our discussion, I would like to introduce myself so that you may gain insight into my motivation, and my related perspective as a cancer patient, survivor, and advocate.

Words from My Father

When I was 13 years old I lost my father, at the age of 43, to lung cancer. It was a dreadful ordeal to see him -- once athletic and muscular -- slowly wither away, a captive of the agonizing, convulsive, and uncontrollable coughing spasms that characterized the last few years of his too short life. His cancer was relentless -- ushered in after smoking three packs a day of non-filtered Camel cigarettes from the days when he was a teenager. At the time of his diagnosis, my father's cancer was a veritable death sentence -- the malignancy had metastasized to numerous other parts of his body, and he was given six months to live.

Notwithstanding the stark reality of his brutal diagnosis, my father reached out to me with his love and communication during the months before his untimely death in a manner he had never done before. Even as his body inexorably withered, his emotional awareness and sensitivity flourished in a way that allowed him to transcend his emaciated physical state. My father was able to connect with me, his youngest son, in a fashion that elevated our relationship way beyond what it was when he was healthy.

Clinging by the thinnest of threads to the life he had remaining, my father explained to me, in his simple, yet eloquent way, that the quality of our life is more important than how long we live. He went on to remind me that the manner in which we live and conduct our affairs is, in the long run, far more important than how long we are on the planet. He told me that, although there were many things he would like to have done, everyone must die someday. Whether we have 3 months, 3 years, or 30 years to live, it is all relative -- life goes by in the blink of an eye.

He spoke, from memory, of Ralph Waldo Emerson's famous quote:

"One of life's illusions is that the present hour is not the critical decisive hour, write it on your heart that each day is the best, the most crucial day in all the year."

About This Book

> *"A thousand moments lost because you took them for granted, just because you expected a thousand more."*
>
> -Saleem Sharma

Great strides have been made in the last few decades regarding the physical treatment of cancer. New methods of operation, radiation techniques and the application of promising chemo and immunological therapies have brought about dramatic improvements in prognosis, extensions of life and even ultimate cures. However, little attention has been paid to the catastrophic and potentially crippling mental consequences of cancer that can rob the individual of his/her enthusiasm and hope, ultimately compromising the ability to enjoy life fully and without fear. This book focuses on the mental aspects of cancer -- more specifically in dealing with the pervasive fear that can consume the cancer patient or survivor -- the obsessive worry that can be debilitating and actually impede your ability to successfully cope with the course of everyday life.

We will work on replacing whatever negative, energy-sucking, emotional challenges you may have, to help you turn them into an opportunity that propels you forward with courage and optimism. We will focus on your attitudes, enthusiasms, hopes, fears, and expectations to marshal your positive mental resources so that you may optimize your chances for a successful journey through the cancer experience and beyond. We do not make a guarantee of survivorship or cure but, rather, promise a way of living meaningfully whatever your prognosis. Your cancer can be a starting point for a constructive re-examination of your priorities and attitudes that can lead you to even greater fulfillment and a life full of positive expectation.

The mind-body techniques advocated in this book represent the latest in neuroscience and cognitive behavioral psychology techniques for mobilizing your inner resources for fighting cancer and for engaging in life positively. Of course, you cannot always predict your cancer outcome, but you can and should be ready and willing to deploy your optimal inner resources to enable the best outcome that you can imagine. Your attitude can make an enormous difference in your experience with cancer and can even be a decisive factor in your survival. Our hope is that, above all, you do not let your fear of cancer choose your destiny.

Throughout this book, I advocate that, regardless of your cancer prognosis, you live your life in the "now"— fully, passionately, and with gusto. Ironically, in order to embrace the concept of "living life fully," we must accept the reality of our own mortality. Regardless of whether you are healthy or not, denial of death, our unalterable life journey's end, can be ultimately frustrating, fraught with self-deception, and insidiously counterproductive. On the other hand, when we contemplate the inevitability of our own mortality, "someday," regardless of our cancer outcome, and accept its reality, we can begin to cherish the priceless opportunity that our remaining time on the planet represents.

We can choose to squander our remaining time and resign ourselves to ultimate futility, or we can deploy what time we have left to enhance the quality of our lifetime experience and to live bravely, fully, and with passion. In this way, cancer can represent an enormous opportunity. We can strive to make our relationships and actions empowering for ourselves and others, as my father did, or we can passively resign ourselves to a negatively anticipated decline. This decision by each individual is volitional -- it is subject to our conscious will -- and is ultimately at our discretion: we can choose to embrace the process and love the adventure of the journey, or we can curse our misfortune. Preeminent social psychologist, Eric Fromm said: "To die is poignantly bitter, but the idea of having to die without having lived is unbearable." Successful living, as I conceive the process, celebrates the fact that life is finite and underscores the priceless nature of the time we have left. We must always remind ourselves that we do not have unlimited time. Indeed, the finite nature of life enhances and accentuates the intensity and excitement of our existence. Today really is the first day of the rest of your life!

I have addressed this book to cancer patients, survivors, and their advocates. Although the techniques and observations we espouse apply to everyone, and all types of anxieties and fears, those who suffer from cancer, with all its implications, are at a particularly poignant juncture in their life's journey, where an enhancement of attitude and perspective can provide an extraordinary opportunity to navigate this life stage optimally. We can see our cancer experience as an opportunity to strengthen and enhance our personal relationships and cultivate significant accomplishments, or we can dread the stereotypical physical and lifestyle decline commonly associated with this nefarious disease.

What About Future Physical and Mental Ailments?

To some degree, we must depend on our good fortune to be spared a cancer catastrophe, and indeed, other poor health and/or mental and physical disability in later life. These variables are only controllable to a certain degree. Of course, we will do well to optimize our prospects through healthy diet, exercise, supplements, meditation, or other legitimate holistic means. In various sections of this book, we discuss the significant proactive steps we can take to optimize our access to optimum medical and ongoing emotional support. But no matter how much we prepare, we must acknowledge that, when it comes to our ultimate outcome -- there can be no guarantees -- we have no choice about the existence of these challenges.

Instead, in these pages, we will concentrate and emphasize that which is volitional on our part, and that over which we can exercise ultimate control: our attitudes. We will accentuate a process for dynamically adjusting our individual mindset and predisposition to our cancer status. We will explore the enormous beneficial effect that our own personal attitude can have on our ultimate navigation and, yes, even enjoyment of this poignant life challenge. The potential to upgrade our attitude represents a tremendous resource that we all can tap, if we are willing to extend the effort.

This book is intended to represent a rejoicing, a celebration of the many benefits and blessings that can be obtained from the examination of our own "inner space" -- our contemplative, detailed review of our unique, personal attitudes and beliefs, both positive and negative, that have a profound effect on our own particular brand of happiness, regardless of our cancer status. We will discuss at length the potential for self-engineering a constructive, personal orientation towards a successful negotiation of our cancer challenge that will ultimately enhance and optimize the experience. Throughout, I will allude to my own experience to illustrate, from a personal perspective, the critical role that attitude plays with respect to the challenges that a cancer diagnosis presents. In particular, we will explore the potential for "re-engineering" our inevitable fears in a manner that provides the optimum opportunity for facilitating future and present quality of life, irrespective of our cancer. This book is intended to be a "hands-on, how-to" guide for individuals who are committed to navigating the cancer process, while not eschewing their passionate participation in the rest of their life. From a practical standpoint, we will discuss how you can take the cognitive behavioral concepts we discuss and apply them directly to your own life situation and circumstances, for your immediate benefit.

Michael Landon, the beloved movie and TV actor who died at the age of 51 from pancreatic cancer, once said:

> "Somebody should tell us... Right at the start of our lives... That we are dying. Then we might live to the limit, every minute of every day. Do it! I say. Whatever you want to do, do it now! There are only so many tomorrows."

How to Use This Book

I have written this book from the perspective of one who has had to contend with the pervasive fear of cancer, for several decades, on all too many occasions, both with respect to myself and my loved ones. I know only too well, the agony and consternation that a cancer diagnosis can bring. Out of my cancer adversity, I have applied the best evidence-based cognitive behavioral psychology principles that neuroscientists have developed in dealing with worry, anxiety and depression. I have used these techniques to lift myself up and feel enormously privileged to share with my brothers and sisters in the cancer community how to use these same techniques to overcome the persistent dread that so often accompanies a finding of cancer. This book is a practical, realistic, self-help work that leans heavily on cutting-edge behavioral science. I have tried to capture, in as human terms as possible, the inherent fear of the cancer journey, and the overwhelming delight of overcoming that fear.

In this book, I would like you, my fellow cancer sufferers, and your caretakers, counselors and loved ones, to learn how:

- A cancer diagnosis can represent an opportunity to reach for the gusto in life, in spite of your cancer challenge!
- Regardless of your situation, to free yourself of the pervasive fear that a cancer diagnosis carries; and to
- Utilize the "Cancer as an Opportunity" Protocol, developed in this book, to create a profound, personal growth experience that will assist you to resume living your life to the fullest and to savor and embrace every precious moment you are given.

I am not implying that the journey from pessimism to optimism is a straightforward proposition, or that it can take place without serious personal commitment. Indeed, to extract maximum benefit from the self-help exercises, you must be willing to engage your own heart, soul and intellect on the path to emotional recovery and emancipation from the negative cycle of anxiety and depression that, all too often, can be engendered by the cancer experience. I do not ask you to blindly accept the Cancer as an Opportunity Protocol therapeutic steps. On the contrary, throughout this book, I have attempted to explain the detailed and informative conceptual precepts that underscore the relevant methodology.

How You Can Apply the Unique "Cancer as an Opportunity" Self-Help Protocol

As you wind your way through this material, you will be provided detailed instruction on how to create a positive mental experience that has been orchestrated to enable you to move forward as you find the energy and insight to envision a constructive cancer outcome. The carefully engineered exercises are informed by cognitive behavioral psychology "best practice," evidence-based models that are customized for the individual living within the shadow of a cancer diagnosis.

These techniques include mindfulness meditation, guided visualization, and mind-body integration. They are each easily acquired, yet powerful tools for tapping into the mental resources that are available to complement your ability to overcome your fear of cancer. They will also help you to live more fully and passionately than ever before. Collectively, they represent a magnificent resource for effectively coping with the negative mental aspects of cancer.

Mindfulness meditation is a simple yet powerful tool for breaking the cycle of chronic unhappiness. It can help us to sidestep the mental habits that lead to anxiety and depression, so we can face life's challenges with greater resilience. Mind-body integration and its concomitant, guided visualization, are cognitive behavioral techniques where an individual is guided to intensely imagine a relaxing outcome or series of positive experiences. Numerous clinical trials have demonstrated that an individual vividly visualizing and imagining a scene reacts as though the event were actually occurring. Such imagined outcomes can have a profound effect on reinforcing positive behavior. Guided imagery therapy has been shown to be effective in helping individuals learn to modify their behaviors by controlling negative emotions in response to perceived threatening situations. Such therapy has been particularly successful with a variety of populations in dealing with all kinds of phobias, anxiety and depression disorders.

The Cancer as an Opportunity Protocol employs the imagery process to intervene in the worry, anxiety, stress and depression repetitive loop that characterizes a pervasive fear of cancer. As part of the Protocol, individualized scripts have been provided to assist you in deploying vivid imagination to overcome worry and anxiety. You are encouraged to feel free to modify the suggested visualization script, as appropriate, for your own circumstances. The goal is to help you develop the mental resources that can support you as you contend with the various challenges that your cancer diagnosis can present. Numerous trials have demonstrated the beneficial effect that a positive mental attitude exerts on the healing process.

You are encouraged to explore each of the guided visualization experiences in this book by reading through the suggested script and immersing yourself in the imagery. You may then record the script yourself, request a friend or support person to read it to you, or you may order the related soundtracks that have been professionally recorded. If you have decided to record the customized scripts yourself (focused more specifically on your personal circumstances), be sure to leave pauses between the individual suggestions so that you can allow sufficient time to develop the imagery. If someone else is reading the script to you, you may signal them when you need more time to experience the suggested image. This can be an extraordinary opportunity to bond with a caring support person.

Before we are ready to undertake the exercises, we will thoroughly discuss the relevant behavioral psychology principles, based on the latest neuroscience, regarding how the human mind processes worry, anxiety, and depression. More importantly, we will learn how to apply this understanding to assist in changing your pessimistic cancer mental outlook to one based on optimism and opportunity.

In Appendix B, you will be given guidance on how to use your PC, or other "smart" device to create personal, customized guided visualization and mindfulness meditation recordings featuring the sound of your own voice and distinguished by your own individual circumstances. The goal will be to learn how to apply your own individualized, self-help, exercises to radically improve your enthusiasm, optimism and zest for living, despite your cancer situation. In the optimum circumstances, you will be supported by an empathic partner, counselor, clergymen or other committed caretaker. However, even if you are relatively alone on your cancer journey, you can still be nurtured by the sound of your own voice, recorded to capture the essence of your personalized, meaningful visualizations that can provide you with enormous comfort, support and commensurate empathy. You can be one of your own best friends. If, despite my encouragement, you lack the time or the confidence to make your own recordings, professionally recorded versions can be obtained at the Cancer as an Opportunity website. Regardless, you will have a tangible opportunity to upgrade the status of your mental disposition and travel as far as you desire away from cancer driven pessimism to an outlook grounded with optimism and enthusiasm for the many blessings that your life still has to offer.

Just like physical exercise, constructive mental exercises, such as the ones described in this book, can be practiced daily to ensure and perpetuate a sound, holistic, and well-balanced life view, regardless of the adversity with which you may contend. The individual, customized mindfulness and visualization recordings that you will be encouraged to prepare, can be enormously beneficial, from a sound mind perspective. At the same time, they are pleasant and designed to be enjoyed. Given the preponderance of modern-day anxiety, stress and worry that abounds in today's challenging culture, especially in the cancer context, you will achieve the greatest benefit by consistently practicing the proactive, positive and therapeutic mental regimen that these uplifting mental exercises can provide.

This book will encourage you to make your own self-help, constructive recordings, narrated in your own voice, to address the pervasive fear engendered by a cancer diagnosis and to overcome the dread of cancer that prevents you from living your life to the fullest. We will teach you how, using your own PC or other smart device, accompanied by readily available background music as inspiration, to employ cutting-edge brain science to create a sensitive, compassionate and effective self-help program that will give you encouragement and valuable, positive support as you process your cancer journey. If you are not inclined to prepare your own recordings, you can still benefit from the professionally engineered recordings that are available at the Cancer as an Opportunity website.

Written by one who has "been there and done that" in dealing with the morass of anxiety, stress, and depression that can characterize the cancer experience, our Protocol is uniquely designed to provide a breath of fresh air in what may otherwise be a bleak, cancer dominated, emotionally dreary landscape. Your consistent use of these state-of-the-art cognitive behavioral techniques will start you on your way towards replacing your current pessimism with a more enthusiastic, hopeful mindset that will allow you to access the precious, zestful life force -- a life force that can inspire you to embrace your circumstances and renew your joy of daily living. At the very least, you will gain insight as to how dread of your cancer circumstances -- the unfortunate "new normal" -- can be replaced with a far more proactive, positive life outlook. At the best, you will vanquish your fear of cancer and transform your pessimism into optimism with the recognition of the many gifts and pleasures that still exist for you to savor starting today!

A Surfing Lesson

My own personal medical history includes a bout, some 25 years ago with bladder cancer, various intermittent skirmishes with skin cancer - an unwelcome consequence from years of surfing under the intense Hawaiian sun -- and, most recently, a diagnosis of high risk, locally advanced prostate cancer for which I have undergone the removal of my prostate and, as an extra bonus because my cancer was considered "aggressive," seven weeks of concomitant radiation therapy. I would like to briefly share with you some personal anecdotes regarding my journey.

I was first diagnosed with bladder cancer at the age of 35. In many ways, prior to my cancer diagnosis, my life had been a celebration of what is possible. I owned my own national CPA firm, was a nationally recognized expert witness in complex financial litigation; was invited to testify before the U.S. Congress as an expert on banking matters; was a prominent author, lecturer, and trainer for numerous government regulatory agencies and industry trade groups, with a beautiful, loving wife and the father of three lovely daughters. As a forensic accountant, I was at the top of my game professionally and newly elected as the president of the National Council for Self-Esteem, a California-based nonprofit whose directors comprised a Who's Who of prominent self-help psychologists and renowned educators.

After graduating from college at the age of 20 with a degree in mathematics I had moved to Hawaii, where I taught at the Kamehameha Schools, an elite private school for Hawaiian students, and pursued my main avocation and passion at the time -- big wave surfing on Hawaii's famous North Shore. Dealing with monstrous waves that found their way down from the Aleutian Islands to pound the shore at Waimea Bay, where I lived with 12 other surfers in a two-bedroom house, I was no stranger to abject fear -- in fact, we sought it out.

One day, while my documentary film partners were filming giant Waimea Bay waves breaking at more than 30 feet, I found myself in the middle of the bay with a group of inveterate, hard-core surfers (a number of whom are surfing legends today). All of a sudden, the horizon filled with mammoth waves that were somberly, and inexorably, marching towards us. Aghast, we bobbed on our surfboards under the dazzling Hawaiian sun, preparing for a momentous and violent event. The waves were "closing out," and way too big for us to successfully ride. Helicopters circled above, and hundreds of spectators, up from Honolulu, were expecting to see breathtaking rides, as well as -- to be sure – the catastrophic wipeouts that would inevitably occur. To be caught "inside," as one of these giant waves crashed down, was a truly harrowing experience. I was the last person "outside" that day and, therefore, furthest out from the shore. Unlike the modern era of big wave surfing, there were no jet skis available to pluck us from danger and transport us to the relative safety of the ocean channel.

As the huge waves lumbered in and filled the horizon, I paddled desperately up the face of wave after wave, hoping to get over each colossal swell before it broke into massive, chaotic turbulence that could hold me down, and spin me around, underwater, for what would seem an eternity. I found myself climbing up a spectacular wall of angry, churning sea -- fearing to go over backwards, to be slammed to the ocean floor, and -- with lungs gasping for air -- my body desperately seeking the surface for a fresh gulp of oxygen before the next wave relentlessly pounded in, bringing yet more chaos and disorientation.

If the Richter scale measured fear, my fear would have been a 10 as I desperately stroked to climb over the waves before they would devour me. After barely negotiating my way up what seemed like a dozen of these monsters, I realized, muscles screaming, that I was at the end of the set. No more waves would be coming for a few minutes and the ocean surface took on a relaxed, deceptive, calm. I had frantically paddled out past the point where the freakish waves would break. Eerily, I was all alone -- the two dozen top surfers who, only moments before had been in the lineup with me, had all been caught inside by the giant waves. Their surfboards had been ripped away and they were forced to find their way to shore through the roiling surf and surging riptide. My stomach churned, and adrenaline gushed as I realized there was no way to paddle in, since the waves were so gigantic they were even breaking in the channel, which normally provided a safe avenue to the shore when things got too gnarly. As helicopters hovered above, with their TV cameras cranking, and cars lined the highway to see if I was going to drown, I made the calculated decision to take off on the first wave of the next set, even though it was too big to ride safely. I had no choice. Two thirds of the way down the face of the behemoth wave, I lost my balance and was slammed towards the floor of the ocean. Lungs screaming for air, and powered by adrenaline, I made it to the surface only to be pounded by the next giant wave that pushed me with explosive force past the shore- break and, eventually, to the safety of the beach. When I finally staggered in, feeling like I had been run over by a truck, I was greeted by a young man who presented me with a large piece of my surfboard that had washed ashore -- it had been broken in half by the massive wave.

The Author at Waimea Bay, Hawaii, with Broken Surfboard

The urgent "fight or flight" fear that I had experienced that day at Waimea Bay, along with the accompanying surge of adrenaline, was typical of the primitive fear with which humans have had to contend since prehistoric times. The sensation of that fear was vividly experienced physiologically in my body and in my mind. Characteristically, this fear was short-lived and bathed in a cacophony of action oriented, stress-induced emotion, the result of myriad chemical reactions taking place in my brain and throughout my body. This type of physical and emotional stress has been experienced by humans throughout the ages. It is the result of the "fight or flight," survival aspect of our reptilian brain. But for this emotional and physical "prompting," my body would, otherwise, not have been able to respond appropriately to the physical requirements of the situation.

In this book, we will talk about another, more insidious, type of fear and emotional stress -- the pervasive fear of cancer and death that, unlike the short-lived, thrill-seeking, physical fear I experienced at Waimea that day long ago, can last for days, months or even years, while it sucks the energy out of our lives and wreaks havoc with our normal zest for living. I have experienced this latter type of fear, also, and it is far more formidable than the fear I faced at Waimea.

I would like to join hands with you to contend with the challenge of the fear of cancer. The reward for successfully facing this fear is enormous and can provide us with an opportunity for a life of fulfillment that my father so vividly described to me when he was on his deathbed. I am sure my father would agree with me when I say that we block our opportunity when we allow our fear to grow bigger than our confidence. And the mastery of confidence and optimism can be learned and facilitated, as we shall see.

Chapter One

Fear of Cancer

> *A mind focused on doubt and fear cannot focus on the journey to victory.*
>
> -Michael Jones

Among those who must endure it, a cancer diagnosis brings almost universal fear, frequently accompanied by shock, numbness and disbelief. The cancer victim's mind can be overwhelmed with having to process more information, emotion and catastrophic imaginings than it can possibly handle. Often, the cancer patient is stunned and dazed -- their minds clouded with dark forebodings and, as actor Angelina Jolie put it, "a deep sense of powerlessness." For many, there is an ominous perception that their life is forever changed, and they are tortured by anxious questions centering on: "What happens if my treatment doesn't work?" "Am I going to die?" and for those who have already received treatment: "Will my cancer recur? "What did I do to deserve this catastrophe? -- Will my life ever be the same?"

Despite significant advances in treatment, cancer is still a word that we have all been brought up to dread. The disease is everywhere and seemingly unavoidable. Indeed, one in three persons suffers from cancer of one type or another -- unfortunately if it doesn't affect you, it affects someone you love. I am certainly no exception. Exacerbating the fear issue, cancer may not be a one-time event. Often, after a period of remission, or ostensible cure, this insidious disease can come back to rear its ugly head a second or third time. Cancer can even become a chronic illness that never really relents. The good news is that, with modern medical technologies, recurrent cancer can often be controlled, and the patient may live for many years. The bad news is that coping with the anxiety of intermittent or recurring cancer can bring on a whole new set of fretful concerns for the patient: When a person has had numerous different treatments, it could mean that the cancer has become resistant to all treatments. When he/she has tried everything, and nothing seems to work anymore, the patient must weigh the benefits of a proposed new treatment that often carries dreadful side effects along with it, without any real promise of cure.

While recurring cancer does not necessarily imply that you will die, this fear is nonetheless something that will inevitably occupy at least the back of your mind. Indeed, worry about cancer and its consequences can be a major negative aspect of the cancer experience.

In 2008, the Institute of Medicine ("IOM") of the National Academy of Sciences issued a comprehensive report that indicated cancer providers often fail to adequately address the psychosocial needs of their cancer patients. The groundbreaking report outlined an optimal model for providing psychosocial care built around the cancer survivor's need to deal with pervasive worry, anxiety, stress and depression relating to ongoing cancer treatment as well as fear of recurrence. A subsequent IOM report noted the general lack of treatment effectiveness for anxiety, depression and overall distress with a take away message that balancing comprehensive cancer psychosocial patient care was made especially challenging because of the limited hospital resources typically available. The report noted that, especially for community cancer centers, the development of programs that deliver effective psychological support for cancer patients often seems "unattainable." Recognizing this pervasive need, the American College of Surgeons, which accredits cancer centers, declared that after 2015, all comprehensive cancer centers had to have an on-site psychosocial program to identify distressed patients and triage them to appropriate care.

This book, which presents and explains the Cancer as an Opportunity Protocol, has been prepared as a cost-effective self-help guide to address this need for positive, comprehensive psychological intervention in the cancer setting. It has been designed to positively address, from "A-Z," the various psychological challenges, including the worry, anxiety and depression that can overwhelm and confound the typical cancer patient and cancer survivor.

Not only is pervasive, destructive worry inimical to your lifestyle, it can also be a negative factor in the success of your treatment. Even when there are no physical symptoms, you may worry and fret over things that *might* happen. As we shall highlight when we discuss the anatomy of worry, *constructive* worry can be very useful to the extent that it provides an incentive to understand your disease -- What are the best available treatments? -- Who are the best available physicians? -- What financial planning may be necessary? -- What lifestyle adjustments may be required, and so on. But once you have used your worry to create an optimum plan of action, you need to let your worry go. This is because additional *destructive* worry can be counterproductive and obsessive -- creating a vicious cycle where it is frequently difficult or even impossible to get off the anxiety merry-go-round. Such habitual, destructive worrying can rob you of your joy of living. And along with it, your possibilities for living your life fully without the pervasive stress and anxiety imposed by your cancer encounter.

Obviously, hope and optimism are important aspects of optimum cancer psychology. No matter how serious your prognosis -- whether your condition is terminal or simply represents a "bump in the road"-- you have the option to embrace the rest of your life and love the adventure of the journey, or you can curse your cancer misfortune. But changing your attitude from pessimism to optimism can be daunting, especially if you are trapped in a vicious cycle of *destructive* worry that can become repetitive and habitual, interfering with your ability to savor current opportunities and experiences. Unfortunately, most people cannot just snap their fingers to create a 180° mood swing from a pessimistic outlook to one reflecting optimism—it takes perseverance and commitment. However, it is one of the most rewarding things you can do.

If you are uncomfortable with the extent to which fear and anxiety relating to your cancer may restrict your enjoyment, or worse, may have taken over your life, this book is for you. It has been written and designed by one who has "been there and done that" on the cancer merry-go-round, experiencing fear, anxiety, and ultimately, freedom from the negative grip that a cancer prognosis can engender. This book is designed to help you overcome the dread of cancer that prevents you from living your life to the fullest. We will discuss how cancer can actually represent an *opportunity* to those who wish to embrace the life experience enthusiastically and with passion. I will describe, in detail, how you can implement the tools of modern cognitive behavior psychology that will allow you to overcome negative attitudes and thought patterns and to generate new positive habits that will create optimism and allow you to be all that you can be, despite your cancer condition.

This book will provide detailed explanation and guidance on how you, depending on the degree of your commitment, can create your own self-administered Protocol to not just change the way you *think* about your cancer diagnosis, but how you feel about it. Positive *feeling*, not just *thinking*, is the key to changing cynicism, pessimism and futility into optimism and enthusiasm for life. I am excited and privileged to take this journey of self-discovery with you. Before we can begin devising your own personal plan to transform pessimism into optimism, we must understand and illuminate the basic principles of psychology that underscore our insights, and which will help you to trust the process.

The Anatomy of Worry

There is an epidemic of worry in America. Anxiety and stress, the unfortunate byproducts of destructive worry, are the most common cause of suffering, and often lead to chronic overeating, use of drugs, alcohol, smoking and even suicide. Moreover, stress and anxiety can lead to, or exacerbate, chronic illnesses such as heart disease and, of emphasis here, cancer. Anxiety manifests as painful distress and is activated by chronic, habitual self-destructive worry. Anxiety and worry can become repetitive and result in incessant rumination about frightful, threatening, and unpleasant things over which we have no control, and which ultimately cannot be resolved by us, no matter how hard we try. In many instances, we worry about things that never will come about. The ability to distinguish between constructive worry, which can lead to the resolution of a problem, and counterproductive, destructive worry, that engenders needless fear and anxiety, can be a learned habit that leads to greater joy, fulfillment and success in life.

An understanding of the anatomy of worry is particularly useful if you are struggling with the prospects of a cancer diagnosis for you or for a loved one. Among adult Americans, fear of cancer is one of the most pervasive sources of anxiety and -- despite advances in cancer treatment -- the fear is for good reason.

Trading depression and anxiety for peace and joy is clearly desirable; but to cancer patients who are besieged with chronic, destructive fear, the metamorphosis from negative to positive outlook represents a substantial challenge that requires focus, commitment and conscious effort. Before we can envision and implement an optimistic future, we must find a way off the repetitive, self-destructive fear merry-go-round that results when we create a vicious cycle of worrisome thinking about our cancer -- anxious thinking that leads to fearful emotions that leads to even further fearful thinking.

Chapter Two
The Author: Who Is This Guy?

> *A pessimist sees the difficulty in every opportunity; an optimist sees the opportunity in every difficulty.*
>
> -Winston Churchill

This book represents a uniquely personal journey: I am writing it as much for myself as well as for all my brothers and sisters who have ever been, are, or will be, afflicted by cancer. To be clear – I, myself, have suffered greatly with all the worry, anxiety, and stress that a cancer diagnosis implies -- based on a good deal of my own past experience. My confidence in the positive outcomes I advocate for all cancer victims and survivors is unequivocally grounded. However, the process is much like a psychological muscle that needs to be exercised and applied regularly. I routinely practice the principles espoused in our Cancer as an Opportunity Protocol myself -- on an ongoing basis. For me, it is a consistent source of satisfaction and personal growth.

My life has not always been a "bowl of cherries." I have certainly had my share of disasters and personal catastrophes. My mastery over my inherent fear of cancer was not the result of any contemporary epiphany – it was not the outcome of some random process -- rather, it has been the result of an ongoing journey and the logical conclusion of the application of mindfulness, self-help psychological insights and exercises that I have relied upon for some time -- since my teenage years. These tools are available to any rational thinking, motivated individual that is committed to positive life experience. We will thoroughly discuss each of these techniques and exercises as our discussion unfolds throughout these pages and how to apply them to your cancer situation.

My own life story serves as a testament to the power of the contemplative examination of preconceived self-sabotaging beliefs born of my childhood where both parents and my little sister died within the span of three years -- and the extent to which our attitudes, out of adversity, can be fortified and upgraded to become a significant force for personal empowerment. Notwithstanding a reasonably happy childhood, where good grades, individual athletic accomplishments and satisfying friendships were the norm, the death of my parents while a teenager launched me into a period of overt delinquency. I went to juvenile court five times (mostly for fighting) prior to the age of 16 and was told by the judge that, but for my good grades in high school (which I hardly deserved), I would be going to reform school.

At the time, my pugnacity was such that, at the age of 13, shortly after my father's death -- as a freshman -- I waded into our high school varsity football team (which later won the New Jersey state big-school championship) and, in a rage, challenged *everyone* to a fight. Later that day, after school, in front of nearly 200 of my classmates, three members of the football team, one by one, accepted my challenge and proceeded to throttle me thoroughly, but not before I split the face of a 220-pound linebacker named "Chase" who then picked my lightweight body up over his head and threw me to the sidewalk, blood spurting from where my forehead had struck the pavement. The remaining members of the football team took pity (apparently, not wishing to go so far as to kill me) and brought me into the varsity locker room where they cleaned up my gushing head wound. This singular event sealed my reputation as a "crazy kid/bad-ass" for my remaining high school experience (despite going "0 for 3" in my individual skirmishes) and foreshadowed a lost three years where, after the death of my mother, I was described to my court appointed guardian, by an examining psychiatrist as: "The most alienated person I have ever seen outside of a mental institution."

Fortunately for me, at approximately the same time, I was introduced to the intellectual notion that, through the power of one's own positive attitude, great, constructive change can be derived. I was fortunate to become familiar with, and an avid student of, the positive, contemplative behavioral, psychological, emotional, mental and philosophical principles that we discuss throughout this book and which have been incorporated into the Cancer as an Opportunity Protocol. More importantly, I was able to apply such precepts, values and exercises to my life's journey -- beginning a lifelong quest for personal growth and meaning. For me, this is an itch that resists all scratching.

In this book, we explore the application of such positive emotional, motivational, psychological and philosophical principles to nurture the successful management of your own growth process, with particular application to the challenge of cancer. We will discuss specific "how to" steps for you to help transform your own, fears and insecurities that, understandably, pervade the cancer landscape and, to the greatest extent possible, convert them into a positive, constructive and holistic approach to the rest of your journey on this magnificent planet. We will examine mental health and anxiety protocols from cutting-edge institutions like, among others, the University of California San Francisco Medical Center and the University of Chicago Department of Psychiatry and Behavioral Neuroscience and see how they can be applied to rehabilitate the worry, anxiety, and depression that often accompanies a cancer diagnosis.

Miraculously (from my perspective), I was fortunate to move forward from my bleak teenage dysfunctional interlude (a "bump in the road") to a life fulfilling and rich with rewards, meaningful relationships and personal accomplishments. Every step of the way, regardless of the situation, a mindful, positive, self-help psychology allowed me to approach the significant challenges and opportunities with an attitudinal power generated from within. This power of a positive and constructive attitude is a gift that can be applied by anyone to lift you up by your own bootstraps and turn your adversity into opportunity, and even greatness. Indeed, that was the secret weapon that allowed me to persevere, and even thrive, despite numerous tribulations, so that like an oyster, I could heal my personal wounds with a pearl.

From my troubled high school experience, I went on to receive a degree in mathematics at the age of 20 from the School of Mines in New Mexico. From there, I moved from the mainland to Hawaii, where I became a big wave surfer and producer of documentary surfing films that were shown in many different locations throughout Hawaii and California. Later, after becoming a certified public accountant, I became an expert witness in complex financial litigation and advisor to some of the largest financial institutions in the world, while forming an international trading company and nationally recognized forensic accounting firm. I have written several books at the request of major publishers on banking and financial matters and am a senior fellow at a prestigious Swiss "think tank" in Geneva, where I spoke at the UN regarding the financial crisis and global financial reform. I am also senior advisor to a large University in Beijing, China and the co-author of a book on entrepreneurship that has been translated into Mandarin and distributed throughout mainland China where I was a primary advisor regarding a major project to provide Internet connectivity to the 700 million Chinese living in the rural provinces. I also managed to come in third at the world mountain biking championships held in St. George, Utah some 10 years ago.

My intent is not to boast or brag but, rather, to underscore the power that a constructive personal attitude plays in shaping our behavior and, ultimately, our life's destiny -- even when, like me, our own life beginnings are not that auspicious. This same attitude can be applied to the challenge of cancer and the related fear and dread that clouds this intimidating life circumstance. Significantly, we as individuals possess the power to modify and upgrade our deeply entrenched beliefs, fears and attitudes and to transform our lives, thereby, in a dramatically positive fashion, regardless of the circumstance. I will allude throughout these pages to my personal journey from dysfunction and fear to fulfillment in order to illustrate and emphasize, from my specific, individual perspective, the behavioral precepts that are discussed.

Through contemplation, introspection and the application of sound behavioral psychology principles, I was able to transform my own attitude and, therefore, my life, from that of a parentless, incorrigible delinquent -- angry at the world -- to one filled with personally fulfilling achievement and relationships. Of course, I failed more than my share of times; but my relentless, self-administered toolkit of psychological and emotional bedrock principles kept me on track. It was my own internal guidance system, my compass, that became a source of strength that I could access as appropriate. My desire was like an arrow that propelled me forward despite inevitable disasters. My aspiration, in highlighting the transformation process I went through, is to reach out to others who are struggling with their own very personal demons and suggest an alternative to anger, indifference and cynicism, particularly in the context of cancer. Now is the time to begin the mindful enrichment that will upgrade your journey as we explore the adventure and challenge represented by a cancer diagnosis. The challenge is to integrate this ostensibly catastrophic circumstance seamlessly into our life plan, without sacrificing any of the related passion, enjoyment, and contentment to which we are otherwise entitled.

The ability to grow from adversity is, in my view, the most powerful human characteristic. This priceless attribute is available to all. Here, our focus is on the challenge of cancer, but the behavioral principles discussed apply to all of us at any age, and regardless of religious persuasion, financial situation, or other personal circumstance, to enrich our life experiences through greater awareness and receptivity to the limitless potential that exists if we are committed to moving forward with personal growth and empowerment, notwithstanding how dark our personal circumstances may seem at the moment.

Together, we can begin a constructive conversation regarding the opportunities and pitfalls of the cancer challenge and, indeed, the aging process generally. I invite readers to participate so that, collectively, we can allow the life force to lift us as high as we can rise and to be able to say at the end, "I loved the adventure of the journey."

My Doghouse Epiphany

Before we can change our mindset, which is actually the accumulation, over the years, of our various attitudes and dispositions, we must have an idea that captures the imagination by storm, and a definite plan for putting that idea into action. We become what we think about most: this is the key to personal growth and evolution and it is the key to a positive coexistence with cancer that, to be sure, requires an adjustment to attitude and perception. I first became familiar with this challenge in the wake of my own deep-down desire to rescue myself from the teenage malaise that nearly resulted in my being thrown in jail some 45 years ago. I can pinpoint my awakening to a particular incident from long ago which is still etched indelibly in my brain. It is ironic that the idea that inspired me to change my mindset was born out of a disastrous incident caused by my poor decision-making at the time. By reviewing this experience, I hope to draw an analogy with the attitude transformation that can result by us viewing cancer, rather than as an obstacle, as an opportunity to reprioritize our lives and enhance our ability to meet future challenges and prospects.

My personal epiphany occurred during the latter stages of the delinquency that was ushered in by the death of my father. Events came to a climax when I was 16 years old and I, with two of my teenage hooligan friends, set out with plans to break into a local liquor store. Our objective was to rip off enough alcoholic beverage to sustain our appetite for the wild, booze filled parties that, at the time, met our needs for the expression of our particular brand of teenage rebellion and angst. Arriving at the liquor store on foot (none of us were old enough to have a driver's license), Bobby -- my comrade in crime -- proceeded to pick the lock of the liquor store so that we could gain entry to implement our nefarious objective. Billy and I watched in anxious anticipation while Bobby worked on the lock when, seemingly out of nowhere, we were surrounded by police cars with their spinning, rooftop lights flashing impending doom -- not only for our failed liquor store caper, but also because I had recently been warned by the county juvenile court judge that I would be sent to reform school the next time he saw me in his court -- I had appeared before Judge Weinheimer no less than *four* times during the previous two years.

As panic seized my insides, I dashed into a field of knee-deep weeds that was adjacent to the target liquor store, where I dove to the ground to escape detection by the police spotlights that were sweeping over the field. After lying undiscovered for at least a half an hour, I froze in dread as I realized the police were getting out of their vehicles to search the weed field that had been my safe harbor from imminent arrest and detention. I was certain to be found and arrested!

With a burst of inspiration, fueled by my adrenaline driven fear, I leapt over the barbed wire fence surrounding the field, tearing the flesh from my left hand as I vaulted over. Almost miraculously, I came upon an oversized doghouse that was situated by a house some 15 feet from the fence. In a nanosecond, I determined that the doghouse represented my only chance to avoid detection. Accordingly, I squeezed through the diminutive doorway (fortunately, no dog was present) where, after tucking my feet up to my chest, I sat quietly as the police searched for me in the field nearby. In breathless anxiety, I watched as a particular officer walked within 5 feet of the doghouse without looking inside, oblivious to my presence. My relief was indescribable as he walked away. I reckon I spent nearly five hours in that doghouse, afraid to disembark as police cars continued to patrol the area throughout the night, searching in vain for the break-in perpetrators.

But something else occurred as I sat in that doghouse for hours, in fear of imminent detection: I began to dwell incessantly on the predicament in which I found myself. I reasoned that, by all accounts, I had enjoyed a happy, supportive childhood characterized by loving (albeit impassive) parents and a happy, enjoyable and largely successful elementary school experience. How was it then that -- only three years later -- I found myself hopelessly alienated from my mother (who, unknown to me, was soon to pass away) and facing the very real possibility of imprisonment with significant prospects for a life of crime and disappointment. As I sat there, huddled in my doghouse sanctuary, I revisited my childhood as a gentle, loving, and essentially innocent, young boy who had catastrophically been transformed into some pseudo, leader-of-the-pack tough guy, constantly struggling in a futile attempt to deny the feelings of grief and hurt that had come to pervade my teenage existence.

I played this tape over and over again in my head as I waited for the dawn's opening sunrise, when I was compelled to make my escape from the doghouse. I vowed to myself that, if given the chance, I would do everything I could to clean up my act and reject the disastrous path that I had undertaken. It was a critical and irrevocable decision that illustrates the power that each of us as individuals can find in personal resolve. My pledge was as if etched in granite -- a lasting, very personal commitment to my own sanity and well-being. But I had little understanding of human motivation and the process through which cynicism, anger, and indifference can grow to pervade an individual's awareness -- much less knowledge of, any useful procedure to ameliorate or overcome such negative psychological baggage. My lifelong quest for insight and self-empowerment began in those moments where I sat huddled overnight in that doghouse some 45 years ago. I was at "ground zero" in what would become an odyssey to savor the life experience and optimize the opportunity that all of us have for meaningful relationships and accomplishments. My quest continues to cast an irresistible lure, still, today -- even despite my high-risk cancer.

After leaving that doghouse safe harbor at dawn and working my way back home by the river, I was greeted by my distraught mother, who had been in anguish for several years over my insidious transformation from all-American boy to the troubled, cynical and largely-dysfunctional teenager that I had become. Unfortunately, I could not find the resolve to tell her about my epiphany in the doghouse the night before and how the experience had changed my life. Nor could I know, at the time, that my mother would only be with me for another two months -- she died shortly thereafter at the age of 43 from peritonitis. Today, I think of her as a self-sacrificing angel, full of love and patience, but at the time, sadly, there was a gulf between us wider than the Mississippi.

The procedures and insight -- the process -- that I employed to coach and counsel myself out of delinquency and into a productive, fulfilling lifestyle were born of that infamous night I spent, literally, in the doghouse. As I have said, this transformational process is, to me, like a muscle that needs to be exercised regularly, throughout the various stages of my life. Like an old friend, it is a lasting resource that provides me with strength when I am tired and hope when I am discouraged. At critical junctures, I am reminded of these precepts and principles which have never failed to refine and, ultimately, inform the quality of my personal search for meaningful existence. With my recent diagnosis of "high risk" prostate cancer, I lean on these positive psychological precepts, even today, to turn my latest cancer challenge into an opportunity for personal growth and advancement. I look forward to sharing this process with you, the reader.

The Odyssey Begins

After my doghouse epiphany, I was never again to appear in juvenile court and, in fact, I began an almost obsessive avoidance of anything characterized as wrongdoing which, with the occasional exception for what I would characterize as matters of principle, continues to this day. A senior in high school, having just lost my mother, I no longer was interested in drunken sprees, gang fights, or in hanging around with my delinquent friends – who, like me, were deeply troubled. Instead, I began to prioritize my heretofore, largely ignored, academic studies, since I perceived college to be a prospect that held great promise and opportunity for me. Higher education represented a means to initiate a fresh, constructive lifestyle, as opposed to my previous three years which had been singularly counterproductive both intellectually and from the stand-point of healthy personal relationships.

I was accepted at several major universities but chose the New Mexico School of Mines, in Socorro, New Mexico as the place where I would, hopefully, launch my come-back into the realm of sanity and positive life experience. Around that time, I became aware of literature promoting the ability of individuals to improve the quality of their mental health through meaningful personal relationships and accomplishments. In particular, the classic book by distinguished psychoanalyst and social philosopher, Eric Fromm, entitled "The Art of Loving," spoke to me at the level of my soul. In his book, Fromm argues eloquently for the power of love and more particularly, the consummate benefit of giving, in terms of individual happiness and concomitant mental health. Fromm said: "Love is the only sane and satisfactory answer to the problem of human existence," and that: "Not he who has much, is rich, but he who gives much." Such reasoning was at first counterintuitive for me, having spent my previous three years heavily invested in protecting myself from feeling, much less giving, anything. It opened a door for me that has never since been closed. Actress Gwyneth Paltrow put it simply but eloquently when she said:

> You'll never be happy if you can't figure out that loving people is all that there is. And that it's more important to love than to be loved. Because that is when you feel love, by loving somebody. I've learned that you get the rewards of love by giving love.

My friends and acquaintances were shocked when, instead of cockiness, arrogance and braggadocio, I started reflecting a sincere interest in warm, enthusiastic communication with them. This was the result of a conscious, concerted effort on my part, a "180° turn," that transformed my life immeasurably for the better. Some 20 years later, when I had become president of the California-headquartered, state legislature funded, National Association for Self-Esteem ("NASE"), I had the pleasure of working with some of the country's leading thinkers on personal development and human psychology, including the preeminent psychoanalyst, Nathaniel Branden, who shared that: "There is overwhelming evidence that the higher the level of self-esteem, the more likely one will be to treat others with respect, kindness, and generosity." It was from Dr. Branden, and other colleagues at NASE that I was able to refine further certain of the insights on adversity, and the ironic opportunity that misfortune can represent, that will be articulated in these pages.

Back in the day, my metamorphosis from out of the abyss of delinquency and into the allure and adventure of big wave surfing in Hawaii and a successful college and professional career, was driven by the realization that our own limiting image of ourselves is frequently not consistent with reality. Based on the quality of our childhood nurturing, we often come to accept and internalize what I refer to as "self-sabotaging beliefs," that can mentally imprison us. Bruce Springsteen sings a song about a man who finds that he has imprisoned himself in a self-made jail that has "shadows for bars." The prison bars are in the man's head, but he is just as much a captive, as if they were real. As a young adult, I discovered that simply by imagining a brighter future, you take the first step towards its accomplishment. One of my idols, New England 19th-century philosopher, Henry David Thoreau, put it this way: "He who advances confidently in the direction of his dreams, and who endeavors to live the life he has imagined, will meet with success unexpected in common hours."

Therefore, it was no surprise to me when, years later, I discovered that the leading cognitive behavioral psychologists in the world were successfully treating victims of apathy, anxiety and depression with therapies that centered on "guided visualization," or creative dreaming and mental relaxation techniques that allow the individual to, first of all, be mindful of what is real in the present, and then to *imagine* something better. I discovered that I could actually practice being happy! I could practice caring about people and getting along with them. Most of all, I could mentally practice being grateful and *savor* all the many gifts and opportunities that would turn my former abysmal circumstances into a treasure trove of new adventure, passion and opportunity. All I had to do was to remove the shadows in my mind that were my own form of prison bars, keeping me from greater fulfillment, peace, and actualization.

During my teenage odyssey, I discovered that the best way for me to overcome fear is to acknowledge it and make friends with it. Instead of running away, I would accept my fear. Next, I would imagine what it would be like if I wasn't afraid. Through creative imaginings, I would see myself overcoming, in my own way, whatever obstacle was present. It is like the great lyric from the beloved musical, South Pacific: "If you don't have a dream, how you gonna have a dream come true?" I used this technique, among other things, for overcoming fear to go from becoming a beginning surfer in Hawaii at the age of 21 to, three years later, becoming a producer of, and surfer in, big wave surfing films on the north shore of Oahu. Initially, my fear of drowning was palpable. But through creative imagining, I visualized myself successfully riding the giant waves at Sunset Beach and Waimea Bay on Oahu's north shore. By practicing what I had imagined, it became a reality.

The Author Dropping in on a Cool One at Sunset Beach, Hawaii

Twenty years later, when I was diagnosed with bladder cancer (my first of several cancer skirmishes), I was initially horrified and bitterly disappointed with myself. I reasoned that I had made all the commitments to physical fitness, proper eating and healthy lifestyle, so how could I be in this situation? Of course, I was afraid of cancer and I felt like the word "CANCER" was shamefully tattooed on my forehead, for everyone to see. Although, at the time, the notion of Cancer as an Opportunity, had not emerged in my head, I realized that, unless I changed my attitude, I would live in fear and dread for the rest of my life.

Ironically, I had just become the president of the National Council for Self-Esteem, a wonderful consortium of teachers and professionals whose board members were some of the top motivational and behavioral psychologists in the world. I had also been experimenting with a "flotation tank" that my son-in-law had built for me. The flotation tank creates an atmosphere of intense meditation and facilitates guided visualization. Many Olympic athletes and others were experimenting with this medium at the time. My own model had sound transducers that could play Baroque and other inspirational music underwater to facilitate the meditative process.

Several weeks after I had been operated on for my bladder cancer, I was floating in the tank when I visualized (day-dreamed about) myself surfing a large wave off of a beautiful tropical island somewhere. It had been a number of years since my intense Hawaiian surfing experience.

However, I felt in my body that if I could surf a big wave, for whatever reason, my cancer experience would be behind me, in the rear-view mirror, and my shock and fear along with it. Later, when we discuss the mechanics and the conceptual derivation of the Cancer as an Opportunity Protocol, we will see why this visualization had such a powerful hold on me. Within two weeks, my beloved son-in-law, Craig, and I found ourselves in Costa Rica on a surfing adventure that fulfilled all the promise of my flotation tank visualization and moved me rapidly along the path to mental recovery from my cancer, while ushering in a new era of personal fulfillment and satisfaction.

Let's take this opportunity to introduce the Cancer as an Opportunity Protocol for turning your pessimistic attitude towards cancer into something more optimistic and fulfilling. My goal is to create room for pleasure in your psyche, safe and apart from any excessive fear of cancer that you may have. Even more, we would like to take this newly created room for pleasure and expand it into a progressive outlook that widens your horizons and opens your heart and mind to the magical possibilities of life, regardless of whatever your particular prognosis may be. I would like every cancer patient and survivor to live life now, fully and in the present, without sacrificing one more precious moment to the obsessive and all-consuming fear of a cancer prognosis.

Following is a brief synopsis of the Cancer as an Opportunity Protocol for meeting the fear of cancer head-on. For those with a pervasive fear of cancer - and there are many - your fear should never be a reason for quitting; it is only an excuse. The other side of fear is freedom and opportunity; but first you must confront your fears, take an inventory, and accept them before you can put them aside and move forward.

PART TWO

WORRY, ANXIETY, AND STRESS: A CONCEPTUAL BASIS

Chapter Three

Overview: The Cancer as an Opportunity Program

> *"We can complain because rose bushes have thorns, or rejoice because thorn bushes have roses."*
>
> -Abraham Lincoln

It turns out that the mechanism most suitable for initially "disconnecting" from the insidious fear loop that can be created by destructive worry about your cancer is the employment of sound, mind/body-based relaxation and other cognitive behavioral psychology techniques that cultivate calmness and allow you to separate from your cycle of anxiety. Certain of these techniques have been explored and developed at learning centers like the University of California at San Francisco, most notably by preeminent behavioral psychologist, Dr. Martin Rossman, whose book, "The Worry Solution," is a classic on the amelioration of anxiety and depression. Other academic and practicing hubs, like the University of Chicago Center for Counseling and Psychotherapy, inspired by behavioral psychology greats, Dr. Carl Rogers and Dr. Eugene Gendlin, innovated much of the thinking that goes into our "body felt sense" exploration and somatic psychology applications.

Later, we will create a specific program that is customized for you to apply these cutting-edge tools that have been developed in behavioral psychology. Once your mind has relaxed and separated itself from your pervasive fear, we will help you to construct positive guided visualizations that will reprogram your brain to think and react more optimistically. The program we will develop with you is based on the latest evidence-based, mind-body science that will be tailored specifically to priority issues that are present in your current life situation. The program can be altered by you as your situation changes. Put simply, the process will encompass the steps depicted in the following diagram.

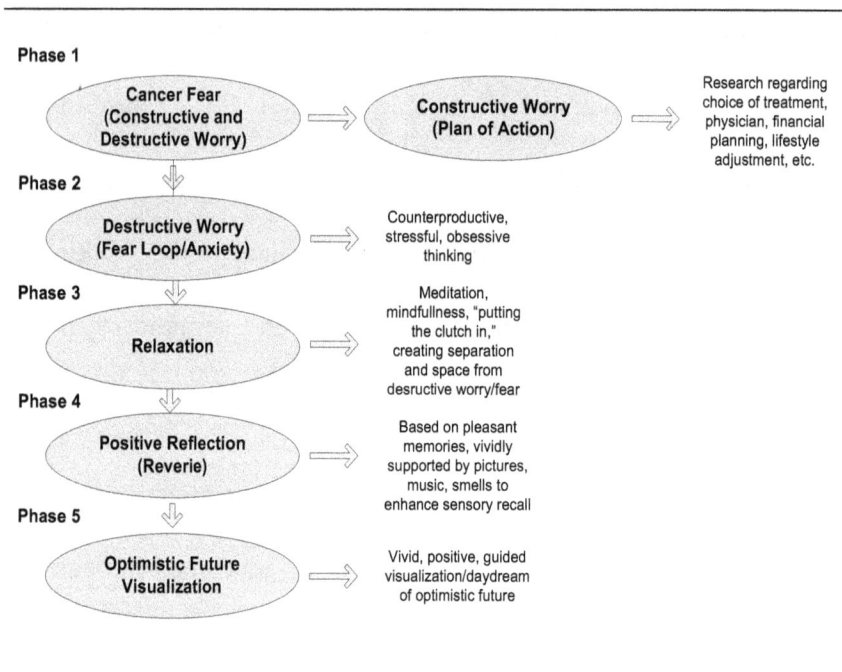

Although this program may, at first, seem complicated, it is based on a straightforward, user-friendly approach that is easy to understand and implement. What follows is a brief overview of the Cancer as an Opportunity Protocol. This introduction will be followed by a lengthier explanation of the process, after we have considered the theoretical and conceptual precepts.

Put simply, if you are in any way driven by your "cancer fear" (Phase 1 in the chart above), then you will be able to take certain tension relieving steps that can begin to shift, and ultimately reverse the initial pathway of worry, anxiety, and physical stress. Of course, initially, "Constructive Worry" should be harnessed to provide motivation for essential research that is necessary to address logistical issues such as choice of physician, medical treatment, emotional support, financial and work issues. This is the first step in the diagram above in dealing with cancer fear. Once you have done your constructive worry and devised a plan of action, any worry that is left is counterproductive and destructive. It serves no purpose for you to obsess, worry or ruminate about issues concerning your cancer that are outside of your control. Having said this, we must remember that there are still many aspects with respect to cancer that we can control, including access to appropriate exercise, diet, treatment and emotional support.

After you recognize that you may be in the throes of cancer-instigated, incessant worry, anxiety, and stress, you need to take proactive steps that provide you with comfort, support and enthusiasm. The second Phase identified in the chart above is "Destructive Worry," which is addressed in our Protocol with "mindfulness meditation," a useful and widely documented therapeutic technique for redirecting your worried mind into an avenue of thought that is more productive: namely, a focus on the present is provided which, at least temporarily, will take you off the anxiety/worry/stress repetitive loop. Later, we will have an entire segment discussing how mindfulness meditation can be implemented and why it is so effective in calming the troubled mind. Another important aspect of dealing with "destructive worry" involves acknowledging and accepting the role played by your fear, so that you can begin to take steps to ameliorate its effect. The acknowledgment of destructive worry and the usefulness of relaxation techniques to climb off the anxiety merry-go-round are dealt with in Phases 2 and 3 depicted in the chart.

The next step in the Protocol, "Positive Reflection (Reverie)," (Phase 4) may not be so intuitively obvious. In weaning an individual from the travails of chronic worry and obsession, cognitive behavioral scientists have found that an instantaneous, 180° turn from an initial ruminative state to a more optimistic, positive state is never achievable. So, in our Protocol, we have inserted an important transition step were the individual is encouraged to recall vividly previous positive experiences (which we call emotional resources) to get in touch with the pleasure centers of the brain that represent the gateway to optimism and more positive thinking. The more vividly imagined, the more helpful the ultimate effect in ameliorating cancer fear. Therefore, we encourage you to experience the positive reflection as much as possible with all your senses, including sight, smell, sound and touch. This may be facilitated by choosing items that stimulate your senses including, if appropriate, relevant music, pictures or whatever else will stimulate or improve sensory recall of the past pleasant event. Special recordings designed to facilitate and enhance your recall can be prepared by the reader, or you can obtain professional recordings designed specifically for this exercise at our website.

Making Your Own Recordings

In a conventional setting, to undertake a mindfulness meditation or guided visualization exercise, you are typically led in person, or in a controlled group setting, by a professional therapist. Alternatively, specifically designed recordings can provide suggestions for you to follow that will guide you in these positive mental exercises. Recordings are available on our website that can help you to relax by focusing on your breathing, or by using some other technique designed to transport you from the cacophonous environment of stressful, everyday living, into a more peaceful, simpler world that is free of the numerous stressful distractions of modern daily life and, especially, a cancer diagnosis. Thus, you can connect with your "inner" self, which is aligned more directly and constructively with your more personal, intrinsic goals. Sometimes, to facilitate relaxation, a recording may play music in the background, over which the therapist speaks. These recordings generally adapt some form of what is referred to by the mental health community generically as "mindfulness meditation," largely popularized by the iconic psychologist/philosopher Jon Kabat-Zinn.

If the therapist wishes to lead you through a guided visualization exercise that will reconnect you to pleasant experiences from your past, you might have an "in-person" session during which the therapist suggests that you go back and search your memories for pleasurable events where you have previously gained satisfaction and enjoyment. Alternatively, the therapist could record a series of positive suggestions on a script that you could follow and to which you could respond, as appropriate, at a time or place convenient for you. The purpose of this recorded exercise is exactly the same as with an in-person session with a therapist -- it is to assist you in connecting with previous positive, life-affirming experiences. To reinforce (anchor) its message, the recorded exercise can be repeated as often as desired. Where appropriate, the cancer patient can pause the recording to gain sufficient time to capture the emotional quality (body felt sensation) from the suggestion relating to the past pleasurable event that has been provided.

The Cancer as an Opportunity Protocol goes one step further and has the reader become his/her own therapist, dictating suggestions on a recording that are customized specifically for the reader's own personal situation. In this book, generic scripts have been provided to support the desired behavioral objective, as outlined in the Protocol chart. In a sense, the reader is undertaking a blended role as therapist and client. This model, which is designed to optimize cognitive behavior, is innovative and unlike anything that has been advocated in the literature. Later, we will walk you through how you may create your own customized, guided visualization recording. For the less ambitious reader, or one who does not have enough time available to make their own recordings, pre-recorded audio of the Cancer as an Opportunity Protocols, including a sample mindfulness meditation audio excerpt, are available at www.cancerasanopportunity.com. They are professionally recorded and will provide the needed direction to accomplish the Protocol goal, albeit without the extra benefit that comes with customizing the approach.

The Cancer as an Opportunity Protocol can assist you to make recordings, with your visualizations, to enjoy and savor as you move forward. We will suggest a script for your meditation or visualization that you will be able to customize to address your own particular situation. As your personal experiences change, you will have the ability to adjust your visualization or meditation recording(s) accordingly. I suggest that you make your own recordings with customized scripts, speaking in a calm voice and pausing where appropriate. Later, I will give you detailed instructions on how to do this. If you do not enjoy the sound of your own voice you can have a friend dictate the recording for you. Alternatively, you may wish to check Appendix C for information regarding prerecorded audio scripts that have been professionally recorded using the scripts included in this book.

When I was in the depths of anxiety and fear, I found that vividly recalling something pleasant from the past was like a cool sponge that wiped clean the toxic residue of fear and anxiety about the future. Later, we will see if it has the same effect on you. In a subsequent section, I will explain how to make a recording of a guided visualization that will help you experience more fully your positive memories from the past.

After reminding yourself how pleasant life can be in the "Optimistic Future Visualization" exercise (Phase 5, above) that follows, you will be encouraged to make a recording that vividly imagines yourself in the future: 6 months, 1 year, 5 years and 10 years down the road, living life free of your pervasive cancer fear, experiencing life fully and with passion.

Of course, some individuals will have a more difficult prognosis than others and, therefore, their challenge and commitment may need to be greater. From a pragmatic standpoint, the worse your outlook, the more that you can benefit from a positive attitude shift. Out of adversity, springs the call to greatness! When given lemons, we shall make lemonade!

You will be encouraged to focus on pleasant, life fulfilling activities that affirm whatever is meaningful in your personal circumstance right now and in the immediate future. Although the process may seem complicated, once you have invested the energy and commitment to take these positive steps in your mind and then breathe life into them through the creation of your own program, you will be rewarded greatly.

The exercises should be practiced daily, for fifteen or twenty minutes, as often as practicable, to reinforce an ongoing change. The stronger your commitment, the greater the benefit. Of course, a competent mental health professional, counselor, clergymen, supportive spouse or friend, can all be invaluable links to facilitate your ultimate success.

Before you can begin building your own, personalized program for transforming your cancer fear (pessimism) into optimism, it will be helpful to examine certain of the principles to be employed in developing your individualized Protocol. Since worry and the fear of cancer consequences are the driving force behind anxiety and stress, we shall take a critical look at the phenomenon of worry, and the complex interrelationship between mind and body emotional experience, so that you will be better equipped to deal with its consequences.

It is our imagination that can create worry and anxiety that distorts reality and can cause us to endlessly ruminate about all the bad things that could happen to us. It is helpful to realize that, more often than not, our dark thoughts are centered on events that will never come to pass. Worry can be constructive and help us to survive. It can cause us to creatively address problems and avoid danger and/or help us to plan how best to resolve a particular problem.

Neuroscientists believe that humans are the only animals that have the ability to imagine the future. This facility of the mind bestows an enormous advantage on humans when it is appropriate to contemplate future events and the effect of contemplated actions that may be taken. However, the ability to imagine the future also comes with a curse, because humans are vulnerable to enormous, unproductive anxiety when destructive worry becomes repetitive and habitual. Dire imaginings of a foreboding future can lead to a kind of hypnotic self-suggestion that exacerbates anxiety and stress. In fact, destructive worry can lead to illness, incapacity, and a general diminution in coping skills.

From an evolutionary perspective, the human brain has been programmed to worry. It can be a source of great stress or abundant creativity, wisdom, and problem-solving intelligence. Through conscious thinking, the choice is ours: whether we allow the brain to run amok with destructive worry, or whether we use our brain constructively as a productive and successful avenue to our success in life. Understanding the anatomy of worry is the first step to harnessing it to our advantage.

Chapter Four
Neuroscientific Foundation for Program Protocol

> *"Hope is the thing with feathers that perches in the soul and sings the tune without the words and never stops at all."*
>
> -Emily Dickinson

What your conscious mind thinks about creates an automatic response from within your body, where your unconscious emotions are warehoused. Thinking about something that arouses fear, like a malignant tumor that may be spreading in your body, can create more worried thinking that, in turn, arouses ever more fear. Simply put, what you feel, you begin to think about, and what you think about most, you feel. When worry is the predominant theme, it can create a vicious cycle where it is difficult or even impossible to extricate yourself from a kind of mental quicksand, where you expend an enormous amount of emotional energy, only to sink deeper into anxiety and depression.

When feelings of fear are aroused by thoughts of cancer, those worrisome feelings often give rise to dark imaginings centered on the cancer, which creates more fear, and so on. It is helpful to have some rudimentary understanding of the neuroscience behind the mind/body connection, and how it relates to your ability to substitute a more appropriate, optimistic emotional response to replace chronic worry and rumination. Although our method will be very personal, it is based on contemporary objective, behavioral science. We will use this understanding of the neuroscientific principles to configure our Protocol to substitute optimism for the pessimistic outlook often associated with a cancer diagnosis, or fear of cancer recurrence.

The following overview of relevant concepts in neuroscience will provide a background understanding for the Cancer as an Opportunity Protocol, which we will be working on together to help you convert your fear of cancer into a more optimistic assessment of your life opportunities and prospects.

Although criticized by a number of contemporary neuroscientists as oversimplified, the most efficient model of the brain to help us understand the fear/anxiety/stress interconnection, sufficient for our purposes, is the famous Triune brain theory developed by Dr. Paul MacLean of Yale University in the 1970s.

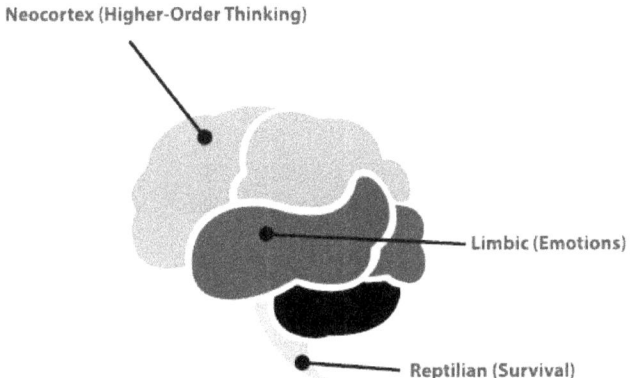

Still used as a model in the classroom to present elementary brain function, the Triune brain model is especially helpful for understanding the application of imagery and guided visualization. Imagery is the key to communicating with your unconscious mind in its native tongue and is the key to communicating with what is otherwise inaccessible. According to this theory, there are three primary sections of the brain that have evolved over time: the neocortex, the limbic, and the reptilian.

The Reptilian Brain

The oldest -- the so-called "reptilian" brain -- controls the body's vital functions including breathing, heart rate, body temperature and balance. The reptilian brain, through the cranial nerves and the spinal cord, communicates emotions as "body felt sensations." The reptilian brain is principally concerned with survival, mating and self-maintenance. It responds reflexively to triggers that relate to "fight or flight issues," and fear situations. Thus, when you have a "sinking feeling in your stomach," because you are afraid, you can thank your reptilian brain. The reptilian brain, which is thought to respond to images, rather than verbal inputs, would originally have been concerned exclusively with issues like: "Can I eat this? Can this eat me? or, Can I mate with this? The reptilian brain is very animalistic and primitive in its nature and is part of your unconscious mind. Its primary role is to make sure that you stay alive and disburse your genes by mating with others. It is your reptilian brain, by way of example, that sends the urgent, albeit irrational, message resulting in your road rage at the driver who has invaded your territory by cutting in front of you. The reptilian brain has a dramatic impact on our basic decisions and can override other, more deliberative, aspects of the brain.

The Limbic System

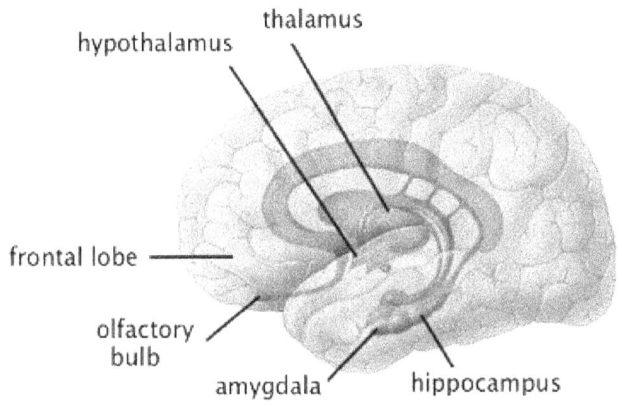

The Limbic Brain

The "limbic," or middle brain, is thought to have emerged in the first mammals. The limbic system processes our emotions and generates feelings when exposed to specific emotional triggers. These feelings create chemical messages that connect information to memory. All memories are enhanced when the information processed has an emotional charge to it. That is why we tend to remember events that create a strong emotional response for us. Because we are largely attracted to those things that bring us pleasure and wish to avoid those that bring us pain, the emotional brain is thought to have evolved to serve and counterbalance the rigid and arbitrary needs of the more primitive, reptilian brain. Thus, the limbic brain will function to ensure that we obtain pleasure relating to basic, essential activities, such as eating and sex, in order to reinforce and support those activities; and that we derive pain from those activities that endanger us -- in order to avoid deleterious consequences. The limbic system responds to imagery and not to language, per se, which is the domain of the neocortex.

Neocortex

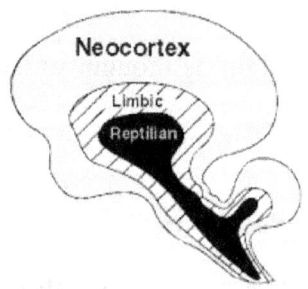

The Neocortex

From an evolutionary perspective, the neocortex is the newest part of the brain and can be referred to as the "thinking" or "rational" part of the brain. The neocortex is the conscious aspect of the three brains, and controls high-level processes, including logic, reasoning, creative thinking and language. The neocortex can be overpowered by the more primal limbic or reptilian brains. For example, experiencing the emotion of anxiety, processed in the limbic system, can result in urgent signals sent to every part of the brain, causing worry, a thought process, in the neocortex and physical stress, a physiological process, which is modulated by the reptilian brain. During occasions of fear, the thinking brain can literally shut down and cause you to react in an entirely automatic, unconscious, and -- all too often, irrational way. The neocortex, the limbic and reptilian brains are interactive and signals travel in all directions. Thoughts originating in the neocortex, become chemicals that engender emotions in the limbic system that manifest as vivid imagery and corresponding "body felt sensations," resulting from chemical signals to the body emanating from the reptilian brain. In a seminal work on the subject, the late Dr. Candace Pert's, "Molecules of Emotion," documents her pioneering research on how the chemicals inside our bodies form a dynamic information network, linking mind and body. Dr. Pert, who was a research professor in the Department of

Physiology and Biophysics at Georgetown University Medical Center in Washington DC., established the biomolecular basis for our emotions. Destructive worry is made up of thoughts that are processed in the neocortex, transformed into emotional anxiety in the limbic brain, and then manifested as physical stress in the reptilian brain.

As noted, the reptilian brain communicates with the body through numerous channels, including the cranial nerves and the spinal cord. Thus, every intense emotion has a physiological counterpart in the body -- a "body felt sensation" that corresponds to an emotional feeling -- giving rise to the "mind/body" paradigm. When you are happy, sad, or calm, you are physiologically very different, and the related body felt sensation varies accordingly. For our purposes, we shall consider that an "emotion" has two parts: 1) vivid imagery that is processed by the limbic system, and 2) an accompanying "body felt sensation" that is engendered by the reptilian brain. Perhaps the simplest example of how this works is to consider a romantic emotion, which conjures up vivid imagery supplied by the limbic system, which is accompanied by unique body felt sensations, courtesy of the reptilian brain. Among other things, numerous biofeedback studies have poignantly demonstrated this connection between the mind and the body.

The connection between mind and body is an important phenomenon, because when reacting to fear and stress -- which, in modern times, is often created by a cancer diagnosis -- powerful stress signals produced by the reptilian brain, and felt primarily in the body, may conflict with a more highly evolved thought process in the neocortex that recognizes, at some level, the damage incurred by destructive, ruminative worry -- about a problem that rational thinking cannot solve. This can leave the individual feeling conflicted and powerless to remove a repetitive, habitual and destructive worry that the neocortex recognizes as counterproductive: for example, a consistent, pervasive dread of cancer recurrence.

In prehistoric times, fear generated by the reptilian brain was typically in response to an immediate threat to survival -- for example, if a predatory animal was about to eat you. Such fear was resolved in a relatively short period in response to an actual, typically physical, threat. For example, you escaped from the sabretooth tiger, or it ate you.

Regardless, in prehistoric times, the matter was resolved relatively quickly. In modern times, the reptilian brain may trigger a stressful, reflexive fear response in reaction to foreboding imaginings about things that may never happen or about which we can do nothing. Such fears may take us over for months, or even years at a time. These "foreboding imaginings" originate as compulsive worry centered in the neocortex and are reinforced by corresponding anxiety in the limbic system, as well as physical stress in our bodies.

Fear Response: Reptilian Brain

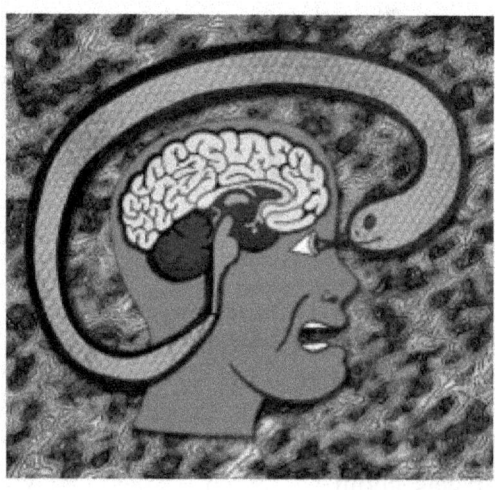

Since the limbic and reptilian brain respond to images, and not verbal cues, the Cancer as an Opportunity program employs vivid imagery in the form of positive guided visualizations, therapeutically, to help shape positive, optimistic emotions and corresponding, pleasure-full, physical responses as antidotes for the destructive worry that may otherwise run amok. Fear of cancer is one of the most pervasive sources of anxiety and stress for modern adults. Once constructive worry has been employed to develop a comprehensive strategy for dealing with related issues and problems, the destructive worry/fear loop becomes counterproductive and ultimately an impediment to happiness and joy in our daily living. The guided visualizations in our Protocol are specifically designed to help guide you over this hump, so that you may reclaim your zest for living, which may have been impaired by your dread of cancer recurrence or other complications of your cancer.

Chapter Five

Positive Guided Visualization: Using Imagination to Change Behavior and Outlook

> *"The natural flights of the human mind are not from pleasure to pleasure, but from hope to hope."*
>
> -Samuel Johnson

Guided visualizations, vividly imagined, can "reprogram" the anxiety that pervades the limbic brain and the physiological stress felt in our bodies as a result of the misguided reptilian brain "fight or flight" response to destructive worry about things over which we have no control, such as the destructive, repetitive, ruminative worry about uncontrollable consequences regarding a cancer situation. Since the limbic and reptilian brains respond to vivid imagery, we will imbue our positive guided visualizations with as much sensory detail, including sight, sound, smell, touch and emotional richness, as we can muster, to "anchor" or "imprint" our self-engineered, positive emotional and physical response to our fear of cancer. You can prepare your own unique imagery in the form of customized guided visualization and relaxation/mindfulness recordings, which you can relate to, based on your own life situation.

To successfully reprogram the intense body felt sensation of chronic fear, the positive guided visualization must be poignant, relevant, and vivid. Reinforced with daily practice, we seek to create a positive thinking/feeling alternative to what was previously a negative fear loop. In this way, we can help to recapture what the French refer to as "Joie de vivre," or our "joy of life." This technique has exerted a powerful influence in my own journey with cancer. Its influence has allowed me to deal effectively with my own fear of cancer and generally permitted me to embrace my time on this planet with hope and enthusiasm, notwithstanding that my cancer could have recurred at any time during the past three decades or could recur in the future.

Use of Nurturing Positive Imagery

Nurturing a child heals the inevitable wounds and hurts from the unavoidable slings and arrows that life provides as the child grows. A child develops confidence and optimism when the parent's nurturing heals and ameliorates the effects of a hurtful or discouraging childhood experience. A parent's loving presence, support and encouragement instills a body felt, integrated confidence that enables the child to meet with greater success in dealing with the challenges of life. Positive childhood nurturing facilitates successful relationship building and meaningful achievement skills.

In a similar fashion, adults can nurture to heal adult emotional trauma, including fear of a cancer diagnosis, by using guided visualization to speak to those deep-down parts of themselves that require support and encouragement. As we have discussed, guided visualization is the appropriate medium of communication with those aspects of our mind that produce physical stress, mental anxiety and related worry. In that context, positive guided visualization is to the suffering adult as positive parental nurturing is to the child in need of support. The means of support for the emotionally suffering adult and the child are different, but the effect of the support is quite similar -- a positively reinforced mental aspect more suitable for meeting contemporary life challenges.

Guided visualization is another type of thinking that is produced by the cumulative flow of thoughts based on sensory perception -- thoughts that take the form of pictures, or sensory stimuli that you can hear, feel, smell, or taste at the personal level. Imagery is the building block of guided visualization. Positive imagery is a way of organizing your ideas, emotions, perceptions and interpretations in a manner that empowers you to heal emotional wounds and thereby grow. Imagery allows you to not only see specific pieces of information, but to process them into a whole -- into a context -- that has meaning. An adult using supportive guided visualization can access those otherwise remote or inaccessible aspects of their personal psychology to re-create the nurturing effect of a parent or a loved one providing comfort and guidance to a child. Unhealed trauma and disappointments are buried in the body and are, therefore, nonresponsive to ordinary cognitive language discourse, but these original painful experiences can still be self-nurtured through guided visualization that communicates comfort and support in the form of imagined pictures, sounds, spatial relationships and feelings. It is never too late to nurture yourself!

The difference between rational (left brained/neocortical) thinking and imagery (right brain/reptilian brain thinking) can be illustrated by a hypothetical individual imagining the passage of a train through a beautiful mountain pass leading to a small, rural village on the other side. From the perspective of a neocortical/rational/left brain observer on the ground, the individual cars of the train pass into view, one by one, and are processed visually in sequence with little, or no, emotional content. Processing the same event as a visualization, the individual could see an aerial picture of the entire train and the beautiful mountain pass with the village on the other side. Let's further hypothesize that the village is where the observer was happily raised in childhood, so that we can add warmly remembered music, sights, sounds and smells to the aerial picture, creating an individual body felt panoply of pleasant emotion and sensations. The positive effect of the guided visualization on the hypothetical individual would be physiological, emotional, and rational -- an integrated experience that would facilitate a nurtured response, versus the more clinical, emotionally devoid outcome derived through rational analysis alone. This is the reason why imagery is important to understand -- it is the dominant language of the reptilian/right brain/unconscious human mind. The beauty of a nurturing, guided visualization is that the individual has a theoretically infinite supply that can be provided at any time, on demand. In fundamental ways, the body/mind does not distinguish between that which is vividly imagined and that which is real.

Brain Conflict and Integration

Our brain is in conflict when its three parts are sending conflicting signals. Therefore, the whole brain must be integrated in order to avoid destructive anxiety and stress. Conflict can occur when the limbic and reptilian brains are sending urgent anxiety and stress signals that our neocortex rejects as irrational and ultimately harmful -- but is powerless to overcome. Such conflict within the brain exists, for example, when you are sleepless at 3 AM in the morning, incessantly worrying about something over which you have no control. You may consciously wish to get off the worry loop but are seemingly powerless to do so. If we wish to overcome a counterproductive irrational fear, we must ultimately bring the mind/body into alignment by reprogramming the limbic and reptilian brain through the use of imagination and positive guided imagery, to which these powerful brain centers respond. This is true whenever we are dealing with chronic anxiety and stress -- regardless of the source of worry. It is especially true when the pervasive fear of cancer rears its ugly head.

Because the reptilian brain exerts such a powerful influence that manifests physiologically in the body, much of our work with guided visualization will not only emphasize what you may be thinking, but also your body felt sensation (what you are "feeling" in your body) -- and whether your release and freedom from fear can be felt in your body. It is important to note that simply processing a destructive worry situation through rational thinking is not effective unless the results manifest in an improved emotional situation evidenced by positive limbic imagery and corresponding body felt sensations. Rather than obsessively attempting to "think" your way through a problem or situation that is logically unsolvable, you are better off to simply imagine how you would feel if your problem were solved. For example, instead of being paralyzed by a fear of cancer recurrence over which you have no rational control, vividly imagining how you would feel without this fear can provide welcomed relief from your destructive worry and anxiety. The process used for attenuating a negatively experienced body felt sensation, is different than the rational process we would use to logically solve a mathematical equation.

Brain Aspect: Anatomy of Worry, Anxiety, Stress Loop

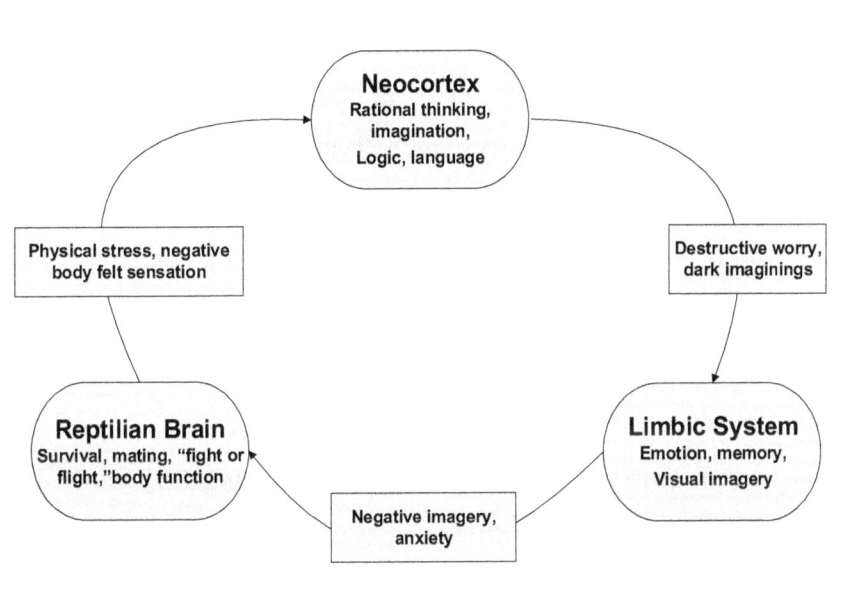

As noted previously, it is possible for rational thinking to go awry and actually become the culprit. It is helpful to employ an analogy to understand how destructive worry as evidenced by ruminative rational thinking (neocortex) may exacerbate anxiety and stress:

Suppose, for example, you are in a fitness room and the simple challenge is for you to travel ten feet from point "A" to point "B." Further, suppose you are standing on a treadmill located at point "A." No matter how fast you run on the treadmill, or how much energy you expend, you will not get any closer to point "B," which is your objective. As long as you are on the treadmill, you cannot achieve your goal. It is not until you get off the treadmill and simply walk from point "A" to point "B," that you will succeed. Similarly, when trying to overcome the anxiety and stress of a destructive worry/fear loop, rational-neocortical, repetitious thinking that employs ruminative, worrisome, imaginings is "much ado about nothing," and gets you nowhere with respect to your objective: that is, climbing off the anxiety merry-go-round. This is true, even though you're trying very hard to resolve the issue with rational thinking. Ironically, you must disconnect from the destructive worrisome (neocortical) imaginings before you can overcome your anxiety. Mindfulness relaxation, which we will discuss shortly, is an appropriate mind/body vehicle for stepping off the anxiety/worry loop.

Although our body felt sensations can be difficult to describe, and descriptions may vary widely, we generally associate a light, airy, warm and comfortable body felt sensation with positive emotions; and tightness, pain, and general irritation with negative emotions. Later, we will judge the impact and effectiveness of our guided visualization exercises, not only in terms of what we think rationally, but just as importantly, how do they make us feel? What is the body felt sensation? Is the body felt sensation consistent with the emotional content we would like to experience? The bottom-line test for whether we have improved the quality of our emotional experience, lies in whether we can "feel" the improvement, as interpreted through a body felt sensation, accompanied by consistent positive imagery from the limbic system. When we experience the body felt sensation that corresponds with optimism and it is accompanied by consistent positive imagery, we say that the three brains hypothesized in the Triune brain model, the reptilian, limbic, and neocortex, are integrated (i.e. no conflict exists) and that the desired behavior modification has been "anchored" or "imprinted."

The powerful reptilian brain finds its urgent "fight or flight" expression in physiological, body felt sensations. The limbic and reptilian brains cannot distinguish between that which is vividly imagined and that which is real. Our goal is to have the reptilian brain interpret the positive, poignantly sensorial visualization as a kind of "all clear" or "it is now safe" signal consistent with a general positive outlook -- and radically different than the urgent fear that a cancer diagnosis can engender. Integration of the neocortex, the limbic, and the reptilian brains, so that no conflict exists between them, turns out to be the key to "anchoring" or "imprinting" personal attitude changes so that they may become lasting, permanent behavioral modifications. This phenomenon is the key to transforming your pervasive fear of cancer into an attitude more conducive to living your life more fully.

Rational Thinking, Emotional Imagery, and Body Felt Sensations
Thinking, emotional imagery, and related body felt sensations are intimately connected -- but, as we have seen, they are not the same thing. All three have a role to play in resolving worry. Body felt sensations that are perceived as pleasant, when accompanied by complementary, pleasurable limbic images (feelings), can produce substantive behavior modification. Constructive thoughts can overcome an irrational fear

only when those thoughts can be translated into positive sensations in the body, supported by pleasurable emotional imagery from the limbic brain. Another way of putting this is that all three sections of the brain must be integrated and devoid of significant conflict. To function optimally, not only must we think rationally, and in constructive ways; but, to be effective, positive thoughts must be imprinted and anchored by emotional images that are complementary to sensations we experience in our body. Rational plans, when internalized and then projected outward through optimistic body sensations and complementary, positive emotional images, lead to goal attainment and, ultimately, success in life! Positive thinking and rational affirmations are inconsequential unless they generate the corresponding, appropriate sensations in our body, along with motivating emotional images that can change behavior. Positive feelings and images are what motivate and propel us forward to take advantage of opportunity, to take risk, and to accept challenge. Our positive body felt sensations and emotional imagery are what truly motivate us: the more passionate, the stronger the motivation. The thinking process can only motivate when it engenders positive body sensations and emotions that support and are consistent with our positive imaginings.

Ultimately, I discovered that the bottom line, acid test for lasting improvement in my fear driven attitude towards my cancer depended on my ability to support my rational action plan, and its positive concept of my prospects, with a palpable, enthusiastic body felt sensation in my body, accompanied by strong, positive feelings supported by vivid imaginings of optimistic, uplifting outcomes. The method for accomplishing this was my use of mindfulness meditation and positive guided imagery to change the way my cancer fear had previously been programmed in my brain. Later, we will discuss, in detail, how you may do the same thing to translate your pessimistic fears into an optimistic projection of your future, thus allowing you more opportunity for love, accomplishment and personal growth for the rest of your life journey.

Rational thinking occurs in response to an emotion -- it occurs in the conscious mind and is, by itself, devoid of emotional content. Every emotion, on the other hand, has a corresponding "sensation" that manifests itself in the body that is supported by complementary imaginings. Thus, expressions like "she has a 'broken heart'," or he is "sick to his stomach," or "my blood turned cold," all describe intense emotions that are felt in the body. The key to lasting, positive attitudinal change is to experience the desired positive disposition in your body, supported by complementary feelings and positive imaginings.

With this understanding, let's have a further, more detailed, look at the Cancer as an Opportunity Protocol and how it has been designed to intervene with, and ultimately overcome, the pervasive dysfunction that characterizes the worry/anxiety/stress merry-go-round with which many cancer victims must contend.

"Cancer as an Opportunity" Protocol
Worry, Anxiety, Stress Loop Intervention

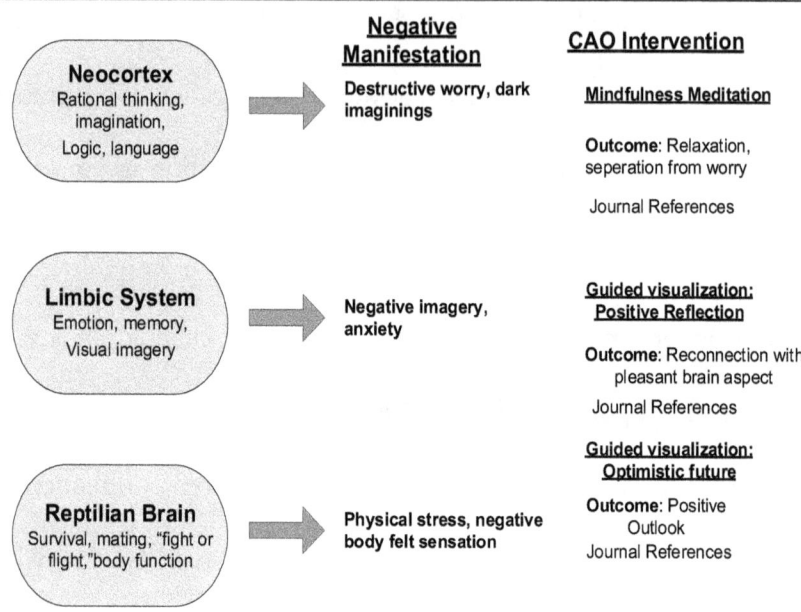

Chapter Six

The Cancer as an Opportunity Treatment Protocol

> *"Ultimately, we know deeply that the other side of every fear is freedom."*
>
> -Mary Ferguson

Earlier, we visited briefly the Cancer as an Opportunity Protocol for changing your cancer fear into a more optimistic, life embracing outlook. Now, we shall delve further into the process to provide an emotional "facelift," and move forward out of any limiting apathy or depression. The Cancer as an Opportunity program for transforming your fear of cancer from a pessimistic into an optimistic outlook is based on the tools of modern cognitive behavior psychology, including mindfulness relaxation, guided imagery and savoring. The goal of this program is to "rewire" your outlook from fear and dread of cancer to one based on optimism and renewed zest for living. The 5 general

Protocol steps are accomplished through a series of cognitive behavioral techniques that are designed to be experienced sequentially in a period of 15 to 30 minutes per session. In order to anchor or imprint the desired attitudinal shift, we recommend undertaking the exercises at least twice a day during periods when you are free from distraction and external responsibilities. You can expect that, after a few days, you will see positive results, although you may wish to continue the daily exercise over an extended period of time. It is a pleasant and empowering interlude that is a positive mental complement to physical exercise, which we also recommend. We will examine below a more comprehensive discussion of the Cancer as an Opportunity Protocol in order to provide some preliminary insight into the therapeutic process and expand on our previous discussion. Later, we will go into much more detail regarding how and why the program works, and what you can do to enhance your own individual experience.

At the very least, the program should provide you, as a cancer patient or survivor, with a source of calmness and perspective -- at best, it will transform your life in a very positive way! The degree of your commitment will, to a large extent, determine your success along with confidence and faith in your ability to improve. Both desirable aspects, your commitment and your confidence, can be supported through gaining and appreciating an understanding of the behavioral rationale for the tools you will use to bring about your positive change. After introducing this conceptual basis, subsequent chapters will delve into detail for the reader who is interested in understanding the theoretical, behavioral science precepts that enable the transformation from pessimism into optimism. Such an understanding can enhance the process and provide insight into how the practice can be customized on an individual basis to deliver maximum benefit. Motivated individuals will wish to follow up on this. The Cancer as an Opportunity exercise Protocol is diagramed below.

Cancer Fear: Transforming Pessimism to Optimism Protocol

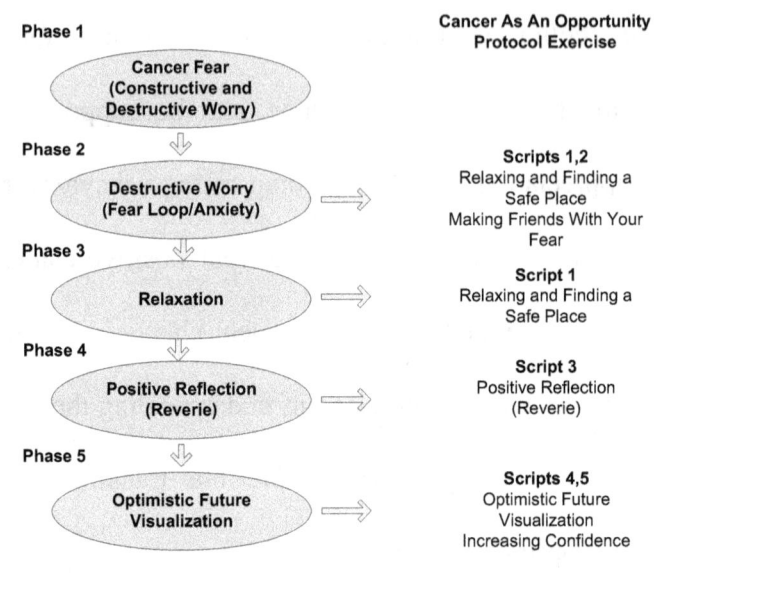

Phase 1: Distinguish Between Destructive and Constructive Worry

If you consider yourself to be in the destructive grip of a repetitive cycle of worry regarding your cancer diagnosis or related fears, the first step is to identify the options available to you for treatment of your own cancer situation. The more you can understand regarding the latest medical tools available to manage and cure your condition, the better you will be equipped to navigate your way through the entanglement of therapeutic and logistical considerations that your condition may entail.

Decisions regarding what physician or physicians are best suited to treat your situation, from both a technical and a personal perspective, are obviously key. You should be encouraged to get second opinions whenever critical alternatives need to be evaluated. Remember that radiation oncologists and surgeons have notoriously different opinions regarding the optimum cancer treatment depending on their discipline. You should feel free to ask the medical practitioner for relevant data to support a potential treatment alternative. You will also be challenged to navigate through your financial situation including, not only medical insurance coverage, but implications for being out of work and any other necessary financial planning.

Lifestyle adjustments such as transportation logistics, physical exercise, diet and other ancillary issues should be evaluated and planned for, ahead of time. Sources of emotional support including spouse, family, friends, support groups and therapists are also an essential consideration. Once you have taken the time to think carefully through the logistics of your situation and are satisfied that you have an action plan that best meets your needs, you should implement the appropriate actions, and then give your worry a rest. Being intellectually and emotionally engaged in your treatment and rehabilitation process is highly recommended. But once you have used your constructive worry to develop an optimum plan, you will wish to take specific steps that will help you cope with repetitive destructive worry regarding your cancer.

Phase 2: Contending with Destructive Worry, Anxiety and Stress

Our brains have been wired for worry since prehistoric times and, but for the importance of rational worry in deriving solutions for problems that can be solved through a cognitive process, destructive worry can engender a negative cycle of unnecessary, habitual suffering that can rob the cancer patient of their zest for living. If you feel that you are experiencing inordinate stress and anxiety from your cancer, the first step is to be able to recognize and acknowledge that you are engaged in a counterproductive, ruminative thought process that does not serve your needs.

Ironically, you need to recognize and accept the extent to which your fear of cancer has subverted your ability to appreciate the many joyful aspects of daily living before you can take positive steps to eradicate that fear. Later, when we discuss the importance of identifying anxious emotions and the "body felt sensations" that characterize stress and anxiety, we will ask you to figuratively "make friends" with your fear of cancer, as a first step to emotional rehabilitation. Realizing and recognizing that you are more than your fear can be a particularly empowering experience.

It goes without saying that you should seek a supportive spouse, friend, relative, support group or therapist that will allow you to express your concerns in an environment of empathy and encouragement. Such an empathic environment will help you as you undertake your journey of rehabilitation from the dark side to regain your enthusiasm and appreciation for the many joys of living. However, even if you lack such extrinsic support, you can learn to be your own best friend. The Cancer as an Opportunity program is designed to help you nurture yourself, so that you will never be alone. If you are stuck in an incessant loop of destructive worry -- and many cancer victims are -- we will look to modern cognitive behavior psychology for a source of mindfulness relaxation that can provide encouragement and relief. We can think of relaxation as a transport vehicle for disconnecting from a worried anxious state. It is a necessary interim step that will facilitate the effectiveness of the guided visualizations that will ultimately help reprogram your mental outlook on a more permanent basis.

Phase 3: Relaxation/Mindfulness Meditation

The relaxation step in our recommended Protocol is designed to help you, as a cancer sufferer, to wind down from an anxious, distressed state into a mental space where you can at least entertain the notion of a more optimum emotional experience. This will allow you to "put in the clutch," figuratively speaking, and give you a rest from the incessant, repetitive and obsessive ruminations that can characterize a pervasive fear of cancer. Such relaxation is a necessary prelude to reengineering your outlook from one of stress and depression into a more optimistic, positive attitude towards living your life to the fullest. This positive attitude does not imply denial, but, rather, represents a commitment to not just existing with your cancer, but to living your life more fully in the present, with gusto and with passion.

Our relaxation step will deploy mindfulness meditation, which has been demonstrated in cognitive behavioral trials to be very effective as an intervention to reduce depression and anxiety. Many studies have also suggested that mindfulness meditation contributes to a more coherent and healthy sense of self and identity. In a later chapter, we will discuss, in greater detail, the impact of relaxation and mindfulness meditation on overall mental health and the various studies by modern cognitive, behavioral psychologists that demonstrate its positive effects. For our purposes now, we can think of the relaxation step as an optimum way of disconnecting from a worried anxious state, into one that is more open to the positive input that will be provided through the Protocol steps that follow involving positive reflection and optimistic future visualization. These subsequent steps are required to imprint and/or anchor the positive behavioral changes we seek and go beyond passive mindfulness meditation in achieving the desired results.

Phase 4: Positive Reflection (Reverie)

Because most individuals traumatized by cancer are not equipped to move spontaneously from a mental space characterized by anxiety, stress and excessive fear, into an attitude receptive to spontaneous joy, optimism and openness to the positive life force -- our Protocol contemplates a gradual, rather than abrupt, "stepping up" from destructive worry (Phase 2) into an intermediary mental state facilitated by the mindfulness meditation/relaxation exercise undertaken in Protocol Phase 3. Even though the Protocol is designed to be experienced fully in anywhere from 15 minutes to, at most, an hour, it is helpful if the steps are taken sequentially, because each step builds on the successful completion of the previous step to enhance its effectiveness. Relaxation is an interim stage -- part of the logical progression from the pessimism to optimism shift that the Cancer as an Opportunity program is designed to accomplish. The more familiar you are with relaxation meditation, the easier it will be to obtain a relaxed state focusing on the present, to the exclusion of external distractions and stress. However, our goal is to go beyond relaxation and actually replace your negative thinking with greater optimism and a positive expectation towards your life situation. The objective is to celebrate your life, here and now!

The next stage in the attitudinal progression from destructive worry and depression to optimism, is to simply recall your most pleasant memories from before the time that your destructive fear of cancer and related worry tainted your ability to live life fully, free of fear and anxiety. You are encouraged by the Protocol material to revisit particularly pleasant times, experiences and accomplishments from your past, before your fear of cancer came to dominate your emotional landscape. You should seek to savor those experiences that stand out poignantly for you. In Chapter Fourteen, we will discuss cutting-edge findings by neuroscientists, who have created a new model of positive experience based on the psychology of savoring and what factors influence the perception and intensity of a pleasant experience.

Protocol Phase 4, positive reflection, is designed to help the individual that is buried in a vicious cycle of destructive worry, to reconnect with the pleasant side of life, the joy of living that can be obscured by a pervasive fear of cancer. After reconnecting with the joy of life that has been obscured by the dread of cancer, you may then be able to contemplate more fully the notion of what life would be like if you didn't have your fear of cancer. The positive reflection step is the next to the last one on your way from converting an attitude of pessimism into optimism. You are encouraged to facilitate your sensory recall using relevant pictures, music, and other personal accoutrements that will allow you to enrich your experience. The objective is to create a reverie that is richly colored by your own sensorial experience of the past events. You should concentrate on your ability to enjoy and savor, in rich sensory detail, these past experiences. You are encouraged to daydream and use your imagination to recapture the body felt sensation of these past experiences. The Protocol instructions found in this book will lay out a detailed plan to assist you to create your most vivid positive reflection.

Phase 5: Optimistic Future Visualization

The last step in your journey to transform your fear of the consequences of cancer into an attitude that more fully embraces your life journey and ability to experience contemporary joy and happiness, free of pervasive ruminations dealing with your cancer situation, is to visualize in exquisite, vivid detail, yourself in the future, free of your fear of cancer and able to enjoy all of the opportunities and prospects for living your life fully and with passion. Just as with the previous Phase 4, dealing with positive reflection and using your imagination, we will create a vision of what you would like to happen. You will be asked to picture yourself 6 months, 1 year, and 5 to 10 years into the future: What would it feel like to be completely free of your fear of cancer or any related concerns? You will be asked to visualize, with as much sensory detail as possible, how you will experience your primary future activities, whether they be professional, family oriented, vocational, or otherwise, as though you were free of any fear of cancer. You will picture where you will be at in terms of personal relationships, fitness and mental alertness. What will you be doing for recreation and fun? You will be asked to imagine the facial expressions you would have if you were actually there. What would you be doing and what would you be saying? Imagine the sounds you would hear, if you were there. What does this optimistic future feel like in your body? What do you look like? Imagine your most optimistic future as if it were all likely to happen – and savor, in exquisite detail, the pleasures you will have: your personal accomplishments; your pleasant, rewarding relationships; and your gratitude for the full life you are destined to experience.

At first, you may have difficulty visualizing life without the traumatic fear of cancer that may have taken over your daily existence. You may have trouble even daring to hope or to be enthusiastic about your future. However, the more you commit yourself to being happy and you understand that you are in control, the more likely it is that you will come to cherish the priceless opportunity that our remaining time on the planet represents. Since you have used your worry to construct an optimum plan for dealing with your cancer -- from a therapeutic, economic and lifestyle perspective -- you are now free to make a conscious choice to put your fear of cancer on the "back-burner," so that you can emphasize the positive aspects of the opportunities and challenges that are available to you. Otherwise, you might waste precious time ruminating and worried, when you could be celebrating.

Clearly, there is a need for balance: It is important that we make an accurate assessment of our potential, while acknowledging our limitations. Even if we are expected to die from our condition, we can still imagine what it would be like to live life as fully as possible without being paralyzed by fear in the time we have remaining, be it 30 days, 30 months, or 30 years. Remember, throughout history, there has always been one death per person. No one has unlimited time on the planet, so, regardless of prognosis, we will visualize the optimal use of whatever time we have left and seek to anchor that vision. Between our limitations and potential there is a vast expanse of living that is defined primarily by our individual choices -- our decisions are volitional. It is important to remember that by hoping for the best, yet planning for the worst, we are not in denial. By using constructive worry to develop an accurate assessment of our life potential, and a realistic assessment of our limitations, we accept that all life is finite. This fact of nature enhances and accentuates the intensity and excitement of our existence. We can choose to squander our remaining time, put our heads in the sand and resign ourselves to ultimate futility, or we can deploy what time we have left to elevate our game, to enhance the quality of our lifetime experience and to live bravely and fully, with gusto and with passion. The choice is ours. To illustrate this process on a personal basis, I offer the following example to share with you my own personal struggle to overcome my fear of high-risk prostate cancer, and how I deployed the Cancer as an Opportunity Protocol steps to facilitate this process.

Self-Example: My troublesome diagnosis of "high risk," locally advanced prostate cancer originally filled me with dread since, per the cold, callous statistics, the chances of my cancer metastasizing during the next 10 years -- even after my prostate was removed – was better than 50-50. Ironically, I have always felt, from somewhere deep down inside -- however irrationally -- that I am "bulletproof," and impervious to personal catastrophe. This notwithstanding, my high-risk prostate cancer diagnosis rattled my mental cage and caused me, albeit involuntarily, to climb aboard that infamous, repetitive anxiety loop -- fear of cancer -- to which we have referred throughout our discussion in this book. I was susceptible to this even though my life experience has demonstrated, time and again, that destructive, obsessive worry is in intractable enemy to be avoided whenever it rears its ugly head. My rational mind told me that my fear was counterproductive, but I seemed unable to shake it. [Phase 1]

On the plus side, my fear of cancer incented me -- in a constructive fashion -- to investigate the latest prostate cancer clinical trials and related research. While searching the Internet, I became aware of several recent clinical trials where excellent results in reducing exposure to both cancer recurrence and metastasis were obtained in high risk prostate cancer patients, like myself. The trials involved a course of radiation therapy that was administered to the subjects shortly after their prostate was removed in a procedure called a prostatectomy. Since, after carefully analyzing the alternatives, I had elected to have a prostatectomy, concurrent radiation therapy was appropriate for my high-risk situation. Most encouragingly, only one out of forty high-risk individuals in a research study experienced metastasis during the 15-year follow-up period after radiation -- a marvelous improvement over the "50-50" conventional odds that I was facing. I breathed a sigh of relief as I mentally calculated that if these results were extrapolated to my situation, I should have little to worry about.

But here is the part that is hard to understand -- at an intellectual, rational level, this news was tremendously encouraging to me. It meant that, if

I undertook the radiation therapy and things went according to plan, there was only a small chance that my cancer would revisit. Of course, this was very cool. Based on the research results, it seemed I had a good chance to get back to my carefree, pre-prostate cancer lifestyle which, by my standards, was full of excitement, pleasure, and fulfillment. This meant that my life would not be forever changed, as I had imagined. Rather, my latest cancer episode would be reduced to a mere "bump in the road." However, notwithstanding that this new radiation procedure held great promise in my situation, the dread of my cancer continued to fill me with cynicism and fear that was palpably manifested in my body. [Phase 2] As a notorious optimist and positive thinker, my fixation on a negative outcome did not fit well within my skin. Regardless of the encouraging research report, I continued to be shell-shocked and intimidated by my "high-risk" prostate cancer prognosis, even though that fear had much less objective justification. While the promising research news had been processed in my head, it was yet to register in my body. This underscores the point that, regardless of how cogent, or how reasonable our rational thinking may be, the conclusions of such neocortical reasoning can be overridden by the body stress felt when our

Reptilian brains are operating out of primitive fear. Figuratively speaking, my Reptilian brain would have nothing to do with the well-founded encouraging, reasoning propounded by my neocortex, regardless of my careful research.

Put simply, my body felt sensation can best be described as a "sinking feeling in my stomach, with a tightness in my temple area, and a sluggish feeling all over." It was like my cancer fear had invaded every corner of my body and taken me over. Regurgitating thoughts, turning over and over in my mind, were simply reinforcing a circuitous "fear loop" that robbed me of my pre-cancer, ebullient zest for living -- my cherished "mojo." Notwithstanding the good news about the encouraging prostate cancer clinical trial, I was unable to emotionally experience the hope, relief and joy that this news should have given me. I kept thinking: "What if this bad thing happens… Or that?"

[Phase 2, acceptance] It wasn't until, after some time had elapsed and I could sit down, clear my mind and create a relaxed meditative state, that I was able to produce some space between my fear, which had taken me over, and the rest of myself that existed outside of my fear. Instead of struggling with my fear, I welcomed it, and figuratively gave my fear a big hug. In a process that is outlined later in detail in this guide, instead of struggling with my fear, I imagined that I had made friends with my fear, accepted it, and did not scold myself or feel ashamed for being scared of my cancer. In my imagination, I figuratively put my fear of cancer "on a shelf," a safe distance away from me. In doing so, I was no longer afraid. I was able to separate myself from my fear of cancer. I realized that I was more than my fear of cancer. I became aware of the many seductive possibilities and opportunities that were still available in my life -- an entire panoply of worthwhile and exciting activities that life still offered -- but for my preoccupation with my physical condition. I realized that my cancer hardly immobilized me in the present -- which is really the only moment over which we have control. I may have dreaded the prospect of a cancer filled future, but for the present day I was healthy and full of opportunity.

[Phase 4] I allowed myself to remember, in rich, sensory detail, recent peak experiences that occurred before I discovered my cancer -- times that were wonderfully free and enjoyable. I utilized pictures, recalled warm communications from loved ones, and listened to relevant, enjoyable music to recreate the texture, fabric and feel of those optimal events. I allowed myself to relish those past occasions.

Once I had experienced this exercise, I allowed myself to savor what it would be like to be cancer free and vividly imagined, in rich sensorial detail, how that would feel -- what I would be doing in six months, one year, or five years from now if I were cancer free. [Phase 5] Again, I constructed in my mind, with as much detailed sensory aspects as I could muster, all the imagined specifics of these optimum future events. Among other things, I pictured warm travels to favorite places with loved ones, giving a speech in Geneva on one of my favorite speaking subjects (of course, to much acclaim!), winning a Master's mountain bike race, surfing in my favorite spot, Costa Azul, Mexico, and enjoying coffee with loved ones at Starbucks.

I truly felt and savored these vivid, intense, guided visualizations, while a glorious splash of sunny lightness surged through my body, replacing the previous "sinking, sluggish feeling" with a warm bath of sunshine -- I felt as if my body were nurtured by a soft, summer breeze. I had accomplished, at least temporarily, replacing my pessimistic fear of cancer with a hopeful, reality-based and optimistic projection of what life would likely be, once I had my radiation therapy and I was cancer free. In terms of our previous discussion, the three parts of my Triune brain were fully integrated and without conflict. For the time being, this wonderful body feeling nurtured me and gave me enthusiasm for the prospects of the current day. I realized that if I could just anchor this attitude, on a more permanent basis, I would be free of my cancer prison without bars -- and free to experience my life fully as I did before my cancer experience.

That was not my first insight that cancer, instead of being an unconquerable obstacle, could represent opportunity to me. In the past, as it is now, it has been a wake-up call to reorder priorities and commitments that could vastly facilitate my emotional and physical wellness. I realized that, as my father advised so long ago, my quest should not be so much for miraculous healing but, rather, for mindfulness -- the greater appreciation of each delicious moment we have on our planet.

To someone who is absorbed and obsessed with the personal threat of cancer, for yourself or for a loved one, replacing pessimism with optimism can be a daunting task. Yet, in that process lies the key to the light at the end of the tunnel -- the way out of the cancer morass. No matter how serious the prognosis, whether your condition is terminal or simply represents a "bump in the road," we have the option to embrace life and love the adventure of the journey, or we can curse our misfortune. Regardless of how many years we have left, whether we are healthy or terminally ill, we have the *choice* to either cherish, or squander, the priceless opportunity that our remaining time on the planet represents.

Part Three

Personal Implementation of Program

Chapter Seven

Let's Get Started

> *"You can conquer almost any fear if you only make up your mind to do so. For remember, fear doesn't exist anywhere except in the mind."*
>
> -Dale Carnegie

Now that we have got some background on how we may attack our fear of cancer and how to replace it with gratitude and optimism for the precious gift of life that we have left, it's time to get started on your own program. If you wish, you may go back to Chapters 3 and 6, where we have previously discussed an overview of the program and how it will work. You will recall that each of the steps involve either mindfulness meditation or some aspect of guided visualization. The most effective way for obtaining the powerful benefit of these techniques is to be led through the relevant steps by someone you trust who is knowledgeable in applying behavioral psychology and familiar with your situation and inner mind landscape.

In applying the Cancer as an Opportunity Protocol, *you* are the best and most natural person to rely upon as a dependable friend. In this chapter, we will share with you how you can make your own self-administered audio recordings that can be listened to at your leisure, according to your own personal schedule. Just as important, we will endeavor to understand, ahead of time, exactly what the behavioral psychology principles are and how they apply to your situation. In this way, you will be able to modify the suggested scripts and customize them, depending on your own circumstance and need.

If you can commit to make the recordings yourself, I highly recommend that you do so. However, making your own recordings can be time-consuming and frustrating, especially if you do not have the appropriate equipment, time and/or experience. To make it easier for you, I have professionally studio recorded each of the scripts in this book with inspirational background music to assist with relaxation and enjoyment. There is ordering information at the back of the book.

Regardless, having the recordings available to enjoy at your convenience anytime, day or night, can be a great asset and an invaluable aid in implementing the Cancer as an Opportunity Protocol recommended in this book. I, myself, keep a set of my favorite recordings, on my iPhone, and can access them whenever it feels appropriate. As we have conveyed throughout our discussion, any sweeping change from an outlook characterized by anxiety, worry, and physical stress to one of calmness, balance, and optimism, will be enabled by:

1) Utilizing your inevitable fear of cancer constructively, to develop an optimal plan of attack to deal with your physical disease and related logistics;

2) Accepting the fact that your fear of cancer will produce destructive worry; and make friends with that worry so that it does not define you;

3) Using relaxation techniques to escape from your repetitive, potentially obsessive worry loop, so that you may;

4) Reacquaint yourself with your feelings from your pre-cancer past that may be associated with your most enjoyable, pleasant, and, at times, wonderful life experiences; and, finally;

5) Develop a life plan based on a positive appreciation of the continuing opportunities for wonder and delight represented by the precious gift of life that all of us have remaining.

At best, we seek to permanently readjust our attitudes from one of pessimism into an outlook that reflects optimism and opportunity. At the very least, we will gain considerable insight into this process.

We have previously discussed how *constructive worry* can be invoked to use your rational, neocortical thinking to develop a plan of action towards your cancer designed to ensure that you receive the best available medical care and logistical support. You will wish to put your best foot forward, while you contend with numerous challenges, on many different fronts that can sap your energy and your spirit, if you are not vigilant.

In this book, we are addressing the formidable *mental challenges* of a cancer diagnosis that remain even after the medical, financial, and logistical issues have been addressed. Dealing with these mental issues sequentially, the Protocol is designed to initially have you disengage from the chronic, obsessive, and counterproductive worry loop that fear of cancer can engender. Conceptually, this is accomplished by what I describe as "accepting and making friends" with your fear of cancer and utilizing a behavioral psychology and mindfulness meditation, to move your mind from a counterproductive, anxious and obsessive state into one of calmness and acceptance. Once we have accomplished this transition, you will be more open towards the enjoyable and pleasant guided visualization exercises that, while pleasurable, also represent your best opportunity to turn your mind into a constructive pleasure-seeking apparatus instead of one that sabotages you with dark imaginings and a foreboding outlook that dwells on your dread of cancer.

In working with our recordings, you will note that we frequently use relaxation and guided visualization techniques in the same script. To obtain the maximum benefit of the exercises, it is necessary for you to be relaxed and calm. There are three secrets that help to create the receptive atmosphere in your mind that maximizes the results of meditation and guided visualization: 1) deep, slow breathing from your belly; 2) relaxation of the muscles; and 3) peaceful visualization.

Deep Breathing

This type of breathing, also known as "diaphragmatic" or "belly" breathing allows for the expansion of your chest to draw your breath deeper into your lungs. Belly breathing is characterized by the belly rising with inhalation and contracting with exhalation. Physiologically, this form of breathing improves our oxygen retention and also facilitates the elimination of waste products from the oxygenation system. But perhaps most importantly for our purposes, deep breathing engages the parasympathetic relaxation aspect of our autonomic nervous system. This is consistent with an "all clear, safety" mode that characterizes the reptilian brain when it is peaceful and not reacting to stress. To improve your belly breathing technique, hold your breath for a couple of seconds after inhalation and take a bit longer as you exhale. If you are doing your belly breathing correctly, you will notice that your abdomen rises as you inhale and contracts as you exhale.

Muscle Relaxation

Your degree of muscle relaxation responds to the power of suggestion and can be controlled by your positive mental inputs. Muscle tightness leads to the buildup of lactic acid, which is associated with stress and tension, and is inimical to the relaxed, receptive state of mind that is most conducive to success with meditation and guided visualization. Therefore, we suggest that you always find a comfortable, relaxed setting where you can enjoy your recordings without interruption or conflict. Research studies have demonstrated that when people suggest to themselves that their muscles relax, their muscles do, in fact, produce a more relaxed state. Therefore, in the meditation and guided visualization scripts that you create for yourself, there will be suggestions to relax your muscles so that you can access maximum benefit from the exercise.

Peaceful Visualization

To create an atmosphere of maximum receptivity to a guided visualization, it is first helpful to be relaxed, while at the same time, creating an atmosphere of safety, calmness, and peace. You can refresh and replenish your brain, body and mind by simply daydreaming yourself into a tranquil, comforting place that has existed in the past for you or that you may imagine in the present. If you invoke all your senses to capture the essence of this beautiful, safe place, you will have created an extremely effective tool to, not only recharge and replenish your spirit, but also afford yourself the maximum potential to enjoy and internalize a positive guided visualization. Because of this, most of our Protocol guided visualizations are set up to help you experience the calming effect of being in your beautiful safe place, before we go further with the separate Protocol exercises.

Chapter Eight

Relaxing and Finding a Safe Place

Protocol Script 1

> "*I don't run away from a challenge because I am afraid. Instead I run towards it because the only way to escape fear is to trample it beneath your foot.*"
>
> -Nadia Comaneci

Before we examine the script for your first Protocol exercise, it may be helpful to remember that these recordings are creating exercises that, like a physical workout, benefit from repetition and commitment. The more committed you are to undertaking the exercises, the more progress you will realize. I, myself, go through a series of Protocol exercises at least two or three times during the day, whenever I have available time. To me, they are refreshing mental breaks that provide balance, perspective, and inspiration. As you progress, your personal exercises can be adapted to any objective or goal that you set, even after your fear of cancer has been ameliorated.

This first script is entitled: "Relaxing and Finding a Safe Place." In the framework of the diagram that appears on page 64 dealing with "Transforming Pessimism to Optimism," this script will concern itself with Phases 2 and 3 of the Protocol, which are designed to take place after you have used your fear of cancer in a "constructive worry" context to research your plan of action in dealing with the logistics of your cancer circumstance. In Phase 2, we will be concerned specifically with getting you off the anxiety/fear merry-go-round that is typically characterized by a repetitive, obsessive process in your brain (neocortex) where, although there is nothing more you can do from a constructive planning standpoint, you continue to unproductively ruminate and stress over your cancer dilemma.

This script is designed to help you to relax and disengage from the worry loop by focusing on your breathing and, later, separating from your fear of cancer to create space for a more positive outlook. By focusing on your breathing, you not only access the benefits of the relaxation response, but you also take your mind off of your repetitive worry dealing with your fear of cancer. It is impossible to think of your fear of cancer if you are focusing exclusively on your breathing. In this section, each line of the script is followed, where appropriate, by an italicized comment that provides explanation as to the rationale for the text. When you see the "..." (...), this is just to remind you that, when using the recording, you are encouraged to pause for as long as you wish after each scripted suggestion.

Whenever we introduce a new Protocol script, we will always provide an explanation, as appropriate, for where the script is designed to take you. A guided visualization is more than random language. It is designed to achieve a desired behavioral result. The following script is intended to initially soften your fear of cancer and replace it with an appreciation for the joy of living one day at a time, so that you can reconnect with the opportunities that each day may represent for you to embrace loving, laughter and personal growth.

This particular script, "Relaxing and Finding a Safe Place," is utilized as an introduction to each subsequent Protocol script that follows, since a relaxed, peaceful and secure mindset is helpful to facilitate the objectives of the subsequent guided visualization recordings dealing with their respective topics as indicated. Here is the text for the script, with accompanying explanation.

Protocol Script 1:
Relaxing and Finding a Safe Place - Text with Explanation

Relaxing and Finding a Safe Place: Protocol Script 1 - with Explanation

-Let yourself relax in a safe comfortable spot...

> *The first three steps in this exercise are designed to encourage muscle relaxation, which facilitates a stress-free, receptive state of mind.*

-It is okay if you are sitting, or if you are lying down...

-So long as you are comfortable and relaxed...

-Now focus your attention on your breathing...

> *You begin focusing on your breathing to access the relaxation response aspect of the autonomic nervous system. Realize, also, that you are channeling your awareness to your present breathing and away from an obsessive fear of cancer.*

-Take a deep breath and notice fresh oxygen entering your body...

-and when you exhale, feel the release of tension and stress...

-and as you are focusing on your breathing --

-notice how your abdomen rises and falls with each breath...

-Just breathe in calmness and relaxation...

-while you exhale tension and stress...

> *The above deep breathing routine can be repeated as many times as you wish until you feel the peaceful, calming relaxation response manifest in your body.*

-and if other thoughts crowd your mind that is okay...

-just gently turn your focus back to your breathing...

-and breathe in calmness and relaxation...

-while you exhale tension and stress...

> *If you are like most people, your thoughts will invariably stray from focusing on your breathing. This is completely normal and should be dealt with as suggested in the script immediately above.*

-When you are ready, picture yourself somewhere that is safe and beautiful...

> *This is technically a deviation from strict mindfulness meditation, which remains passive throughout the process. Here, we are suggesting a visualization that is designed to calm tension and reduce the stress of an anxious, worried mind that is preoccupied with the fear of cancer.*

-It can be a place where you have experienced contentment and joy in the past --

-or it can be a place that you make up in your imagination...

-Just let yourself daydream that you are in this safe and beautiful place...

> *You may have more than one safe place that comes to mind. There are no rules. Just choose the one that feels right and comes to you most clearly at this moment. Make sure that your safe place visualization creates a feeling of comfort and peace which is experienced in your body.*

-Notice how comfortable your body feels in this special place...

> *Because your stressful, anxious emotions are stored in your body, often at an unconscious level, all our exercises will encourage you to be more aware of how you feel in your body. This can be surprisingly difficult to articulate. Later, when we focus on your fear of cancer, you will imagine what it would feel like to be rid of your anxiety and stress as a first step to overcoming them.*

> *For now, just enjoy the comfortable body sensation of being in your own favorite safe place.*

-Notice any pleasing aromas, sights, or sounds…

> *The more you can use your senses to enhance a visualization, the more effectively it can influence communication with your reptilian and limbic brains, which do not respond to language but, rather, respond to vivid imagery.*

-How do these pleasing aromas, sights or sounds make you feel in your body…

> *See if you can notice how specific stimuli create different body felt sensations.*

-Is there music playing…

> *See if you can notice how specific stimuli create different body felt sensations.*

-Is the sun shining in your special place…

> *See if you can notice how specific stimuli create different body felt sensations.*

-Is it daytime or nighttime?

-Is anybody there with you in your special place?

-Notice how happy and relaxed you are in this safe and beautiful place...

-Notice the calmness and relaxation in your body...

-and if other thoughts crowd your mind, that is okay...

> *It is inevitable that your mind will drift. When this happens, just bring your focus back to your breathing and, when you are ready, resume the exercise where you left off.*

-just gently turn your focus back to your breathing...

-and exhale tension and stress...

-Take some time to enjoy and explore this safe and beautiful spot...

-Breath in calmness and relaxation --

-and exhale tension and stress...

-Notice how this calmness and relaxation feels in your body...

-Let go of whatever may be bothering you in the moment...

> *This is an opportunity to go even deeper into relaxation -- to "put your worry on a shelf, alongside, and separate from you."*

-Just release the tension and stress...

-and welcome the calmness and relaxation...

-Give thanks for this special place where you can relax and be safe...

> *Learning to appreciate and give thanks is a fundamental aspect of "savoring," which, as we shall see later, is a cornerstone of the Cancer as an Opportunity Protocol.*

-and realize that you can always return to this special place…

-Whenever you want, you can experience this peace and relaxation…

-Now savor this feeling in your body…

-Take time to notice how your body feels in this safe place…

-and realize that you can always come back—

-You will always be welcome here.

-When you are ready, you can gently bring your attention back to the outer world…

-But you can take with you to the outer world your body felt sense of peace and calm…

-that is available to you in this special place inside you…

-As you return to the outer world, give thanks for this ability to go inside.

End of "Relaxing and Finding a Safe Place": Script with Explanation

Concluding Comments Regarding This Script

This exercise is a fundamental tool to enable the separation from the anxiety/worry/stress loop that can often be the end-product of "destructive worry" that we have described previously as a characteristic mental side effect of the fear of cancer syndrome. *This exercise can be modified by you to address your own personal situation. For example, you may wish to include description in your script regarding a specific safe place that is special to you, along with specific language to prompt and facilitate your own sensory recall.*

In Appendix B, we will show you how, if you wish, you can dictate your script over an appropriate background music selection and create a professional sounding recording based on your own personal set of circumstances. The script for "Relaxing and Finding a Safe Place," without explanations is reprinted for your convenience in Appendix A, at the end of this book.

Chapter Nine

Exploring Body Felt Sensations

> *"Confront your fears, list them, get to know them, and only then will you be able to put them aside and move ahead."*
>
> -Jerry Gilley

In the previous chapter, we discussed the preparation of a script designed to provide someone with a pervasive fear of cancer with a means for disconnecting from the troublesome worry/anxiety/stress repetitive loop caused by destructive worry, to find a more relaxed and secure state of mind. This exercise forms a prerequisite for the other exercises in the Protocol series which build on this relaxed, secure state to open the possibilities for developing a more constructive, positive based, outlook. Therefore, we recommend that the "Relaxing and Finding a Safe Place" exercise be undertaken as an introduction to each of the other recommended Protocol visualizations.

We introduced the application of two powerful behavioral psychology techniques: mindfulness meditation and the use of guided visualization. In the next section, "Separation from Your Fear of Cancer," we will introduce a technique for working with the "body felt sensations" that are produced by the action of the reptilian brain which, through the cranial nerves and the spinal cord, communicates emotion to the body. This "mind/body" connection plays a major role in perpetuating any type of fear or anxiety, as discussed previously in Chapters 4 and 5. Before introducing the next Protocol script, it will be helpful to review the nature of bodily felt anxiety and stress, and emphasize why addressing such bodily sensations is so critical to transforming your fear and anxiety into a more positive, optimistic and ultimately, life-embracing outlook.

The Nature of Bodily Felt Pain

As pointed out earlier, every significant emotion has its epicenter in the body. Below the surface, bodily felt pain, fear or conflict is typically obscured, obfuscated and overridden by rational, conscious thinking, which is the domain of the neocortex. However, it is this tight, inner, bodily-felt, hurting place that is the real "800-pound gorilla" that can control our most basic fears, desires and destinies. Merely "intellectualizing" and thinking rationally about a significantly negative "sense" in the body does not resolve or provide meaningful relief from the inexorable, energy sucking pain that is stored unconsciously in the body. Although the conscious mind must focus to provide the key to initiating the resolution of negative based beliefs and emotions, any therapy that relies on talk and the conscious mind alone can only provide temporary relief. Prominent psychotherapist and author, Dr. Peter A. Campbell has stated that:

> "… Reason can never make a tight, hurting, inner place unbend! Reason can't get *inside* it! Solutions in the mind are never the same as a resolution in bodily knowing. Reason always remains outside of the hurt which it thinks about."

To find relief and a lasting resolution, one must physically enter into the body felt sense and feel the movement, shift, or release in order to gain relief in the body and true progress towards self-emancipation and empowerment. Focusing on the body felt sensation of a particular "feeling" is a particular process of attention that supports therapeutic change, a process that has been linked in more than 50 research studies with successful outcomes in psychotherapy. First developed by pioneering philosopher and psychotherapist, Dr. Eugene Gendlin, who along with Dr. Carl Rogers conducted their research at the University of Chicago, inspired much of the somatic oriented, mindfulness-based approaches used in cognitive behavioral psychology today.

In an appropriate context, you can experience the feeling of freedom from original pain, anxiety, fear or stress that can restrict your personal expectation for positive things to come. Simply by focusing on a more pleasant outcome through vivid, positively experienced imagery, relief from negatively experienced body felt sensations can be derived. Such a profound "shift" in the body felt sense can provide dramatic resolution that does not come with mere intellectualization. It is important to recognize rationally that a condition or circumstance is being experienced negatively and, therefore, holding us back. Intellectual realization of anxiety or fear locked in the body may be a first step towards its disposition, but it does not represent its therapeutic resolution. Intellectual rationalization can, at best, provide temporary, superficial relief, unless it leads to ultimate resolution at the body (unconscious mind) level. See our previous discussion of "Brain Conflict and Integration," in Chapter Five.

The body is a hugely underestimated, primary domain of human emotional experience. We are not metaphysically just our minds, even though we tend to think of ourselves this way. An emotionally hurtful body sensation must be physically experienced, felt, acknowledged (not run away from) in order to provide contemporary access to nurturing and healing at the deeply rooted, unconscious level. The Cancer as an Opportunity Protocol, in addition to employing mindfulness meditation and guided visualization, applies a different, feeling based, modus operandi to resolve profound anxiety, fear, and stress that are locked into the body landscape. Since the reptilian and limbic brains, the source of much stress and anxiety, respond solely to imagery, a heavy emphasis is placed on experiencing the visualization in rich sensory detail. The Protocol script in the next section introduces these concepts. Much of the body-oriented aspect has been inspired by, and adapted from, the focusing community and, in particular, researchers Edwin M. McMahon, PhD and Peter A. Campbell, PhD and their working paper:

"Focusing Steps: Longform." A brief overview of such technique for body felt sense (emotional) resolution follows:

1. Initially identify the body felt sense that lies just below the surface, inside the body, that prevents us from being really happy;
2. Accept or "make friends" with this scary, hurtful, inner space which we have habitually avoided in the past -- don't run away! This provides a "welcoming" presence, as opposed to the intellectual denial we habitually employ to protect us from that which we inwardly fear most; [Note: This repression of negative emotions at the rational, "thinking" level is well documented in the authoritative, academic and scientific literature referenced at the end of this book]
3. Introduce yourself to the possibility for present, contemporary nurturing -- a different way of experiencing the inner felt sense that is based on a loving, caring presence we can provide to ourselves;

4. Ask yourself: Can you imagine being free of your current stressful issue -- the sense of just letting go? Can you imagine putting your current stressful feeling on a shelf, apart from you? What needs to happen for this whole thing to feel better? Can you imagine the best-case scenario and/or the optimum disposition of this issue? How does all this feel in your body? Can you feel this way all the time? What would that be like? By imagining what it would be like not to have your fear of cancer, you are creating exactly the atmosphere we desire. To the extent that you can identify this feeling in your body, you will have taken a giant step on your journey to softening your anxiety and creating the opportunity for optimism.
5. Savor the body shift – the actual "felt' sense of release and resolution that comes from our nurturing the hurting inner felt sense, rather than scolding or rejecting it intellectually;
6. Memorize the physical feel of the nurtured inner space in order to resolve and replace the hurtful body sense with a new physical sense that has been invigorated with optimism, love, and hopefulness;

7. Whenever the feeling of stress, hurt or dysfunction resurfaces -- don't panic -- take a deep breath -- make peace with the feeling -- and savor the physical feel of the nurtured inner space;

8. Provide thanks for the ability to release or "shift" the experience of the felt body sense from a place of hurtfulness and negativity to one of promise and enthusiasm.

As you can see from steps 4-8, above, the essence of our Cancer as an Opportunity program success depends on your ability to imagine, in rich sensorial detail, what it would feel like to not have your fear of cancer. If you can do this, you can free yourself from the shackles of your compulsive anxiety regarding cancer and begin to enjoy the blessed gift of life that remains, in different quantities, for all of us. Our Protocol scripts are designed to help you get to this cathartic point. It is as simple as that. The incessant, intellectual rationalization that attempts to solve a problem that has no rational solution, such as destructive worry relating to a cancer outcome, is counterproductive and only adds to the vicious cycle of anxiety, worry and fear. Now, let's look at the next section which discusses the Protocol Script: "Relaxation and Making

Friends with Your Fear." This Protocol script is designed to exploit the concepts we have just discussed.

Chapter Ten

Relaxation and Making Friends with Your Fear

Protocol Script 2

> *"Fear is never a reason for quitting; it is only an excuse."*
> -Norman Vincent Peale

In this section, we will explore what it feels like to realize that you can be more than your fear of cancer. This is a very important step in altering your predisposition from anxiety to optimism, because when an individual is obsessively consumed with fear, there is a tendency to let that fear define all aspects of his/her life. While this script, and all of the other Protocol scripts, call for the same "Relaxing and Finding a Safe Place" introduction, in order to avoid redundancy, the script which follows omits the introduction and starts with an in-depth exploration of the body felt sensations of your fear of cancer. You may recognize the Protocol from the discussion in the previous chapter. As always, you should be thinking of how you might customize this boilerplate script to personalize and individualize it to reflect your own circumstances.

After including the "Relaxing and Finding a Safe Place" material discussed in Chapter Eight, which you have already reviewed, you are now shifting your relaxed attention to your body and, more specifically, to where you experience your fear of cancer in your body. Remember, the powerful and often dominating reptilian brain, which responds to sensorial images, translates fear and anxiety into body felt sensations. That is why we use positive imagery in the form of guided visualization to "speak to" this aspect of your deep-seated cancer fear. It is important to identify how your fear manifests as a body felt sensation and to work with the internal body felt sense. Our body felt sensations are typically difficult to describe with language, but they are the key to resolving our worry, anxiety, and physical stress. Fear and hurt that resides in the body responds to positive nurturing just as does rational worry centered in the neocortex. However, the technique for nurturing a toxic body felt sensation is different.

Protocol Script 2:

"Relaxation and Making Friends with Your Fear" – Text with explanation:

Relaxation and Making Friends with your Fear – with Explanation

-Ask yourself, "How am I feeling right now?" Let your body do the answering...

-Ask yourself, "How does realizing that I have cancer, feel in my body?"...

You are becoming aware of a feeling that has been previously experienced in an unconscious fashion in your body. It is a feeling that is typically repressed from awareness because it is unpleasant and scary.

-Ask yourself, "Where do I feel this fear of cancer in my body?"...

Calls attention to the body felt sensation of trauma that was previously unrecognized/unconscious. Note that it is impossible to nurture a feeling that you have repressed deep down inside. Instead of ignoring the feeling, you will learn to acknowledge and accept it, so that you can begin to nurture this place in your body. You must learn to become your own best friend.

-Ask yourself, "In what ways does my fear of cancer stand between me and being really happy?" Let your body do the answering....

> *You are acknowledging the power of this heretofore, largely unrecognized feeling in your body that, nonetheless, unconsciously adds considerably to your stress level. You cannot dissolve an unwanted feeling (fear of cancer) if you refuse to acknowledge it.*

-Is it okay to be with how all this feels, right now? …

-Ask yourself: "How does the worst of this feel inside my body?

> *This step acknowledges the power of this traumatic, stressful body felt sensation and the gravity with which it pulls you down. It underscores the imperative nature of successful resolution. We typically resist doing this, because generally, we are committed to denying our hurtful feelings, as a defense mechanism to prevent us from experiencing our hurt.*

-If this feeling is so overwhelming, that you want to run away from it, then take some time to create an atmosphere of warmth and caring acceptance…

> *Instead of being at war with this feeling, can you make peace with it; can you sit down at the table with it, acknowledging its existence and the profound effect it has on your life. This is the beginning of reconciliation and healing.*

-See if you can treat this hurting place inside with gentleness and kindness in a way that it can feel that presence from you…

This step, and the five steps immediately below, are all designed to help you to begin to dissolve the hurt and the fear. It also helps you to realize that you are more than your obsessive fear and begins a process of objectification of the fear that allows you to think of other possibilities for dealing with it.

-Can you create a feeling climate towards this body felt sensation that is the opposite of the way you usually treat it…

-Is it possible to hold this feeling in your body in the same way you might hold and nurture a hurting child? …

-Can you imagine putting your arm around this place in your body and patting it, or stroking it? …

> *Notice how, in this context, your fear becomes less threatening.*

-Notice where you feel this fear most in your body and place your hand there to comfort, pat and caress it, or just let it know from your touch that you care and that you are present.…

-Can you do your best to become friends with, and accept, your fear? …

> *This concludes your exercise towards making peace with your fear, a first step in dissolving your fear and contemplating an alternative attitude centering on your appreciation for the many opportunities to experience joy, love, achievement and the many benefits of living one day at a time. You have created space in your mind for a new way of looking at your situation.*

In this next section, before concluding our exercise with body felt sensation, we will mount a campaign to overcome the pervasive fear that has been locked unconsciously in your body and replace it with feelings that are more positive. Remember, the reptilian and the limbic brain respond to images that are sensorially experienced, so you will wish to create imagery that involves as many of your senses as you can.

-Now ask yourself, what needs to change inside of me for this to begin to feel better…

> *Begins to acknowledge that there may be an alternative to this all-consuming traumatic body felt sensation of fear. Permits focus on the physical sensation in the body, which is the beginning of a solution.*

-What would feel like a small step forward with all this…

> *Rather than demanding immediate resolution, this presents a calm, patient approach. You are patient -- but will not be denied!*

-What would feel like a breath of fresh air…

> *Creates more space between anxiety producing feelings/sensation and begins to condition your body for a positive resolution. (You are "putting your toe in the water.")*

-Imagine for a moment, how it would feel inside if everything were all okay…

> *Bingo! This is the realization that a solution does exist. Hallelujah!*

-Could you feel this way all the time...?

> *Wow! This would be a complete victory over a formerly all-consuming, life sucking dilemma. Let's imagine how this feels, over and over, in rich sensory detail, until it becomes a conditioned habit. Do this and you will begin to find freedom from your fear!*

-Take time to become familiar with the feel of this changed space in your body so that you can come back to it in the future...

> *You will likely need repetition of this entire exercise in order to effect a lasting change. The more frequently and the more seriously you are committed to practicing this or your more customized version, the more likely you will be to achieve lasting attitude change.*

End of "Relaxation and Making Friends with Your Fear" Script with Explanation

We have just discussed the script for this Protocol exercise, along with explanations, to relax and make friends with your fear of cancer. Once you understand the rationale, you can adjust the wording to suit your own circumstance and preference. The irony in this exercise is that, to overcome your obsessive fear of cancer, you must imagine what it would feel like in your body. Once you can imagine what that would feel like, you can repeat the exercise as many times as necessary to imprint or "anchor" consistent emotional behavior. Instructions for recording, including with soft background music, are found in Appendix B.

Our next exercise will be to create a recording to imagine a safe place that will facilitate your transition into the Positive Reflection, Phase 4 of the diagram, "Transforming Pessimism to Optimism," on page 64. Please note that you will find a full copy of the script for the previous exercise, "Relaxation and Making Friends," dealing with the body felt sensation of fear, in Appendix A.

Chapter Eleven

A Few Words about Guided Imagery

> *"Imagination is more important than knowledge."*
>
> -Albert Einstein

As noted previously, our Cancer as an Opportunity Protocol relies on cognitive behavioral psychology therapeutic techniques, including the use of guided imagery to form positive visualizations that promote relaxation and relief from the pervasive anxiety, worry, and stress that characterizes fear of cancer. Imagery is nothing more than thoughts or mental representations that have sensory qualities.

In the therapeutic community, guided visualization is used to help clients achieve a number of different health goals including overcoming trauma, phobia, and the elimination or reduction of habits that threaten health, including smoking, overeating, and drug addiction. Guided visualization is also employed to provide healing, and/or symptom reduction, for a variety of physical ailments and symptoms including, among other things, dealing with chronic headaches, gastrointestinal problems, high blood pressure, sleeplessness, and chronic pain.

Typically, a therapist leads the client through guided visualizations that are intended for specific therapeutic purposes through which the client can access their own inner (unconscious) resources to reinforce and facilitate their healing process. In the Cancer as an Opportunity Protocol, the reader takes the role of therapist, and the guided visualizations are self-administered through customized scripts that, in a sense, play the role of the therapist. This is not to denigrate the value that support from a therapist or other empathic source (e.g. spouse, partner, friend, clergyman or physician) can provide, but simply recognizes that outside support is not always accessible. Moreover, your personally adapted Protocol scripts and exercises can be accessed at any time and deployed at your convenience. Guided imagery can be used in many different contexts to improve performance and is applied extensively at the elite level in sports psychology. You may find that once you have overcome your fear of cancer, you will wish to continue the positive habit of utilizing mindfulness meditation and guided visualization to enhance many different aspects of your life, on an ongoing basis. The following Protocol scripts have been specifically designed to address the issues in Phase 4 and Phase 5 of the Cancer as an Opportunity Protocol dealing with "Positive Reflection" and "Optimistic Future Visualization," respectively.

Chapter Twelve

Positive Reflection (Reverie)

Protocol Script 3

> *"In a person's lifetime there may be not more than a half a dozen occasions that he can look back to in the certain knowledge that right then, at that moment, there was room for nothing but happiness in his heart."*
>
> -Ernestine Gilbreth Carey

About this exercise

Because most individuals traumatized by fear of cancer cannot just snap their fingers and move spontaneously from a mental state of worry, anxiety, and stress directly into a more positive disposition characterized by enthusiasm and optimism, our Protocol contemplates a gradual, rather than abrupt, stepping up from destructive worry (Phase 2) into an intermediary mental state of relaxation and security, which is part of the logical progression from the pessimism to optimism shift that the Cancer as an Opportunity program is designed to accomplish. To be clear, our objective is not just relaxation, but to go beyond relaxation and displace our repetitive negative thinking with greater optimism and positive expectation on an ongoing basis. Put simply, we are looking for a permanent attitude shift.

As an intermediate step, in moving from pessimism to optimism, we will assist you to prepare a Protocol recording that recalls and revisits your most pleasant memories from before the time that your destructive fear of cancer and related worry tainted your ability to live life fully, free of fear and anxiety. The objective is to create a rich, sensory driven reverie that allows you to enjoy and savor the body felt sensation of these past pleasurable experiences. You are encouraged to embellish your past experiences with your imagination. There are no rules other than that you seek to find your optimal pleasurable state. By reconnecting with the joy of life that has been obscured by your dread of cancer, you will be more open and motivated to contemplate how rich your life can be once you are free of your related stress and anxiety.

In this Protocol script, "Positive Reflection (Reverie)," you will be encouraged to facilitate your sensory recall through the use of relevant pictures, music, and other sensory inputs that will allow you to savor these past pleasurable events to derive optimum benefit. In the Protocol script that follows, you are encouraged to customize our generic visualizations to reflect your own personal experiences in vivid detail. Once you have edited the generic script to reflect relevant sensory inputs, you will then be able to follow the instructions in Appendix B to produce a recording uniquely suited to your own, subjective circumstance.

It should be noted that, even apart from our goal to relieve the anxiety, worry, and stress that a cancer diagnosis can evoke, a regular visit to your own, personal, most enjoyable, emotional and achievement-oriented milestones from your past is highly recommended and encouraged by those behavioral scientists and psychologists who have studied the subject in detail. Later, we will comment at greater length regarding the results of their studies on how savoring past experiences provides positive psychological benefit.

We have printed the Protocol Script for Phase 4: "Positive Reflection (Reverie)" with relevant explanations, where appropriate, immediately below. Note that, as with all the Protocol scripts, you may wish to introduce the new topic with the other (Script 1) material dealing with relaxation and creating a safe space, which has previously been reviewed by you. This introduction is helpful to create a receptive state of mind for the new material. Accordingly, you may decide that only a brief review of the introduction is helpful.

Protocol Script for Phase 3:
"Positive Reflection (Reverie)" with Explanation

Positive Reflection (Reverie) – with Explanation

-As you relax in a safe place let your mind recall how you felt before you were diagnosed with cancer…

-How did that feel in your body…

-Can you remember any past special experiences, special times and special events that you recall with particular joy?

> *You should select an occasion(s) from the past that was particularly pleasurable and satisfying. It can be from your recent pre-cancer past, or even from your childhood. Consider identifying several of these memorable occasions and the particular enjoyable sensory detail that make them come alive for you. For example, is there any song or music that brings back the memories vividly; or pictures; or other unique sensory stimuli? Once you have identified the event(s), have your customized recording ask you the following questions:*

-What was enjoyable about that special event…

-How did that feel in your body…

-Where did you feel that enjoyable sensation in your body…

-Imagine how you would act if you were there at your special event: What would you be doing… What would you be saying…

-Imagine the facial expressions you would have if you were there at your special event…

-Imagine the sounds you would hear, if you were there at your special event…

-What does all this feel like in your body…

-Can you isolate the body felt sensation of that experience and dial it up a notch…

-Can you remember any past special experiences, special times and special events that you recall with special personal pride over your accomplishments?

> *You should select an accomplishment and/or meaningful achievement from the past that was particularly pleasurable and satisfying. It can be from your recent pre-cancer past, or even from your childhood. Consider identifying several of these memorable occasions and the particular enjoyable sensory detail that make them come alive for you. For example, is there any song or music that brings back the memories vividly; or pictures; or other unique sensory stimuli. Once you have identified the event(s), have your customized recording ask you the following questions:*

-What was enjoyable or rewarding about that special event…

-Where did you feel that enjoyable sensation in your body…

-Imagine how you would act if you were there at your special event: What would you be doing… What would you be saying…

-Imagine the facial expressions you would have if you were there at your special event…

-Imagine the sounds you would hear, if you were there at your special event...

-What does all this feel like in your body...

-Can you isolate the body felt sensation of that experience and dial it up a notch...

-Can you remember any past special experiences, special times and special events that you recall with warm feelings of friendship or love?

> *You should select an occasion(s) from the past that was particularly pleasurable and satisfying. It can be from your recent pre-cancer past, or even from your childhood. Consider identifying several of these memorable occasions and the particular enjoyable sensory detail that make them come alive for you. For example, is there any song or music that brings back the memories vividly; or pictures; or other unique sensory stimuli. Once you have identified the event(s), have your customized recording ask you the following questions:*

-What was enjoyable about that special event...

-How did that feel in your body...

-Where did you feel that enjoyable sensation in your body...

-Imagine how you would act if you were there at your special event: What would you be doing... What would you be saying...

-Imagine the facial expressions you would have if you were there at your special event...

-Imagine the sounds you would hear, if you were there at your special event...

-What does all this feel like in your body...

-Can you isolate the body felt sensation of that experience and dial it up a notch...

[Closing]

-Can you give thanks for these special experiences...

Learning to appreciate and give thanks is a fundamental aspect of "savoring" which, as we shall see later, is a cornerstone of the Cancer as an Opportunity Protocol.

-and realize that you will always have these memories and special occasions to remind you of just how good life can be...

-and that you can always return to this special place...

-Whenever you want, you can experience this peace and relaxation...

-Now savor this feeling in your body...

-Take time to notice how your body feels in this safe place and these beautiful memories...

-and realize that you can always come back—

-You will always be welcome here.

End of Positive Reflection (Reverie) Script with Explanation

Additional Comments Regarding This Script

This script has been designed to help you overcome the vicious cycle of destructive worry associated with a pervasive fear of cancer and to reconnect with the pleasant side of life, the joy of living that can be obscured by obsessive worry, anxiety and stress. After getting back in touch with the joy of past pleasurable experiences, you may then be able to anticipate more fully the notion of how much better your life could be if you didn't have your fear of cancer. This positive reflection script is a key step on your way from converting an attitude of pessimism into one of enthusiasm and optimism. You are encouraged to facilitate your sensory recall through the use of relevant pictures, music, and other sensual stimuli that will allow you to enrich your experience. You are also invited to modify the exercises to reflect issues relating to your own personal situation. In Appendix B, we will show you how, if you wish, you can dictate your script over an appropriate background music selection and create a professional sounding recording based on your own personal set of circumstances. The script for "Positive Reflection (Reverie)," without explanations is reprinted for you at the end of this book in Appendix A.

Chapter Thirteen

Optimistic Future Visualization

Protocol Script 4

> *"Here in your mind you have complete privacy. Here there's no difference between what is and what could be."*
>
> -Chuck Palahniak, *Choke*

This Phase 5 script has been designed to help you accomplish a final Phase in your journey to transform your fear of cancer consequences into an attitude that more fully embraces your life journey and ability to experience contemporary joy and happiness, free of pervasive ruminations on your cancer situation. This guided visualization will encourage you to experience in vivid, sensory detail an optimistic future where you are free of your fear of cancer and free to enjoy all of the opportunities and prospects for living your life in the future more fully and with gusto.

Using your imagination, you will be asked to picture yourself in the future where you are totally free of your fear of cancer and any related concerns. You will imagine how you will joyfully experience your primary future activities including professional, family, vocational, recreational, accomplishments and satisfactions. You will also be asked to construct a vivid picture of where you will be at in the future in terms of your personal relationships, fitness, and mental health.

You may have trouble visualizing future life without the traumatic fear of cancer that may have taken over your daily existence. This may be particularly true if you are not sure of your prognosis. For those who may be diagnosed as terminally ill, the reader can determine what he/she would like to accomplish in a timeframe that may inspire greater urgency. However, everything is relative and the goal is still the same for all of us. As far as I know, throughout history the immutable equation has always been: one person, one death. Therefore, we are not seeking immortality, we are seeking mindfulness--the greater appreciation of each delicious moment while we are on the planet. Remember the lesson of my father, whose last six months at the culmination of his life was experienced fully with incredible joy, optimism and dignity.

For those who are not terminally ill, and, also for those who may be, the goal for all of us is to celebrate the joy in living life one day at a time, as completely and fully as we possibly can. We can't go wrong with that approach. Many of us may be seriously challenged by our prognosis – and many will have the realistic hope of a permanent cure -- but with no guarantees. Hoping for the best, versus dreading the worst, is the most courageous, enjoyable and practical choice for all of us. Otherwise, we squander whatever precious time we have remaining. As Mark Twain put it, "I have had a lot of worries in my life -- most of which have never happened."

The more you commit yourself to this exercise, the more you are likely to experience the benefits of your best potential future life, free of excessive worry, anxiety and stress. We have emphasized previously that all life is finite, for everyone, and must come to an end someday. This fact of nature only underscores the intensity and excitement for the remaining time we have left. You have used your constructive worry to come up with the most effective plan for dealing with your cancer challenge. You have not ignored your responsibilities -- you have "taken care of business." So now let your imagination soar in doing this exercise: give yourself permission to set your sights on the optimum appreciation of each potentially delightful moment you have left. Do this for yourself and your loved ones around you. This exercise is intended to be modified by you to address particulars of your own personal situation. Your script can be modified by you in the future to address any changes or current developments, so that you will always have a contemporary life plan based on optimistic imaginings and observations for your personal customization.

Because this section is so intensely personal, a little homework on your part will go a long way towards guaranteeing the effectiveness of this exercise. Work that you have done in Protocol Script 4: "Positive Reflection (Reverie)" will be helpful in providing a customized springboard to the optimum future visualization contemplated in this exercise. In the following script, you will be asked: "Can you savor this feeling in your body?" If you cannot do this, or you do not get the optimum body felt sensation, then go back to the Protocol for Phase 3 and focus on the following prompt (page 171): "Can you remember any past special experiences, special times and special events that you recall with particular joy?" Or: "Can you isolate the body felt sensation of that pleasurable experience and dial it up a notch?" If you are stuck in this current exercise, use what comes to mind from this past exercise to create a springboard towards positive expectation in the future.

As with all the Protocol Scripts, you will be led into the Phase 5 exercise by an introduction involving Phase 2, "Relaxation and Finding a Safe Place." Since you have previously reviewed this material, you may choose to move forward to the bolded material below, beginning with: "Can you picture your future life with more special, pleasurable experiences…"

The Protocol script dealing generically with your optimistic future visualizations follows.

Protocol Script 4:
"Optimistic Future Visualization," Text with Explanation

Optimistic Future Visualization - with Explanation

Note: This section begins the specific material on the "Optimistic Future Visualization."

-Can you picture your future life with more special, pleasurable experiences like the ones you have just savored in Protocol Script 3, "Positive Past Reflection (Reverie)"...

-Just take your time and sort through your previous special, pleasurable experiences...

-Take all the time you want to savor and enjoy these past pleasurable experiences...

-And if you have more than one pleasurable experience, just choose the experience that seems to have the most energy for you, right now...

-See if you can break down your pleasurable experiences into one where you experienced warm emotional relationships and another where you experienced success in accomplishing a meaningful achievement or, perhaps, an occasion where you were moved by an experience in nature...

-And if one pleasant experience stands out, then see if you can locate where you experience this pleasant sensation in your body...

-Just relax, enjoy, and savor this experience as much as you like...

-Can you picture this delightful feeling seeping pleasantly into every cell in your body...

-Imagine that this wonderful feeling projects a soft, warm, invisible light all around you...

-Imagine that other people cannot see this light, but that they can feel its pleasant aura...

-Now realize you are still in your safe place, breathing in calmness and exhaling tension...

-Can you let go of your fear of cancer or recurrence in the future, make friends with your fear, or otherwise put it on a shelf, separate and apart from you and your future...

-And, being in your safe place, comfortable and relaxed, see if you can daydream about having pleasurable experiences in the future one year, three years or five years down the road...

-And now focus on where you would like to be in your personal relationships in the future: what is your expectation for warmth, comfort and commitment in your personal relationships in the next six months, one year, or five-year period...

-What does this feel like in your body...

-Could you feel this way all the time...

-Take time to become familiar with the feel of this changed space in your body so that you can come back to it in the future...

-And now take time to imagine your personal achievements over the next five-year period...

-How do these future achievements feel in your body…

-Can you celebrate the sensual pleasure of these body felt sensations that relate to your optimistic future…

-Can you give thanks for the safe place you have created and the unlimited opportunity for pleasure that you have been blessed with…

-Remind yourself of how quickly time flies…

-Can you practice living one day at a time -- making each day the best…

-Can you savor this feeling in your body…

-Take time to become familiar with the feel of this changed space in your body so that you can come back to it in the future…

-How does anticipation of these future achievements feel right now in your body…

Can you celebrate the sensual pleasure of his body felt sensations that relate to your positive visions for the future…

-Can you give yourself permission to enjoy and savor these pleasant body felt sensations regarding your future…

-And realize that you can always come back to these feelings…

-And that you will always be welcome here in your safe place…

-And when you're ready, you can gently bring your attention back to the outer world…

-But you can take with you to the outer world your body felt sense of peace and calm that is available to you in this special place inside you…

-And as you return to the outer world, give thanks for this ability to go inside…

    End of Optimistic Future Visualization with Explanation

Closing Comments on this Protocol Script

To a large extent, your success in gaining freedom from the tyranny of your fear of cancer is in direct relationship to your level of commitment. In order to compose an effective and purposeful script that will fill you with the requisite inspiration, you will need to take the time to visit our previous exercises and tap into your priceless "inner space" to find out where you need to go. If you have successfully navigated the previous exercise dealing with positive reflection, you will have identified the material upon which you can build a positive expectation for the future.

When I was a boy scout, my friends and I took part in a contest to make a fire from scratch using a piece of flint and a small steel bar. The idea was to strike the steel bar with a piece of flint stone which would cause a spark to be emitted if the steel bar is struck just right. We would capture the spark, if we could, on a piece of charred cloth that was just underneath. If we were successful, the charred cloth would glow from the captured spark that would then spread. Underneath the charred cloth we would have our "tinder," made up of any dry, straw-like combustible material that we hoped to catch on fire. By blowing persistently on the charred cloth on top of the combustible material, the spark would spread and eventually ignite the tinder. In many ways, my search for relief from the dread of a cancer diagnosis was like my flint and steel exercise that I enjoyed so long ago. Although you had no guarantee you could start a fire, if you had the right technical approach with the proper flint and steel accoutrements, and if you were persistent, you would eventually light the tinder to start a robust conflagration. In doing your Protocol exercises, sometimes you will catch a spark in the process that leads to a burning fulfillment and ultimate satisfaction. Other times, you may not be as successful. Persistence, commitment and confidence in the process is a necessary ingredient.

The Protocol exercises that we have discussed on these pages, outline specific steps that I have been able to apply in many different situations, including to greatly assuage my fear of cancer. I have done this on more than one occasion. Fear of cancer can be pervasive and unrelenting. Because it is such a formidable challenge that affects so many people, in so many insidious ways, it gives me great pleasure if I can help you, my brothers and sisters, in the cancer community. But the journey to overcome this imposing fear needs vigilance and practice. You may revisit any of our exercises, any time you feel the need, just as I do. I find that, like physical exercise, positive mental exercise, to be utilized most effectively, requires consistent application of effort. But, like physical exercise, positive mental exercise is a joyful, invigorating activity. As we are coming to the end of our discussion on how to defeat the fear of cancer, I would like to add a few more comments on how you can "kick it up a notch" with respect to your fear of cancer, and life in general, by savoring your best and most positive experiences, to inspire and fortify you against inevitable hardships.

Chapter Fourteen

Kicking it up a Notch: The Art of Savoring

> *"I have always believed in savoring the moment. In the end, they are the only things we will have."*
>
> -Anna Godberson, *The Luxe*

It should be clear that a large part of the secret for overcoming the anxiety and fear of cancer lies in our ability to substitute positive psychology for a more negative approach to life. In the world of positive psychology, the father of research on "savoring" is Loyola University Chicago social psychologist, Fred Bryant. Bryant describes savoring as "noticing and appreciating the positive aspects of life. Savoring is more than pleasure -- it also involves mindfulness and "conscious attention to the experience of pleasure." Many people assume that when good things happen, people naturally feel joy for it. Bryant's research, however, suggests that we don't always respond to these "good things" in ways that maximize their positive effects on our lives. Dr. Bryant, who is the author of the 2006 classic on the subject, "Savoring: A New Model of Positive Experience," is in the process of analyzing numerous academic studies dealing with savoring to determine how we can derive maximum benefit from our own pleasurable activities.

This is exactly the process we are invoking in the Protocol exercise dealing with Phase 4, "Positive Reflection (Reverie)," where we strive to reconnect with our peak pleasurable experiences from the past to remind us of what we may expect if we are living life fully in the future. At the end of this section, we will present an exercise that is designed to help you "dial up" your positive expectations and help you to enjoy this preview of coming attractions in your life. It behooves us to examine some of the primary activities and insights, based on his research that Fred Bryant, and others, suggest will assist us to develop the art of savoring as a skill.

Sharpen Your Sensory Perceptions

Recognize that all pleasure is supported by rich, vivid sensory perceptions. When you are savoring a past reflection or visualizing a future pleasant experience, seek to involve, as much as possible, all your senses. When you are experiencing a rich and rewarding pleasurable experience, be mindful of the body felt sensation -- take a mental picture, so that you can come back and savor the pleasurable experience again. Peak mental experiences are like precious diamonds. They are, by definition, in limited supply. Therefore, celebrate them with gusto and passion. It is our past peak pleasant experiences that fortify and sustain us in visualizing our own optimistic future. Therefore, we should regularly revisit peak moments from the past.

Share Your Good Feelings with Others

Pleasure shared with your loved ones is pleasure multiplied. Sharing our peak moments with others increases our joy. According to Bryant, "Savoring is the glue that bonds people together, and it is essential to prolonging relationships. People who savor together, stay together." When you are experiencing the trauma of a cancer event, friends, confidants, counselors and partners can be an invaluable link towards sustaining a positive, future expectation. Don't be shy about sharing your poignant, pleasurable experiences with others.

Practice Living One Day at a Time -- Make Each Day the Best!

My father, dying from lung cancer, with six months to live, shared with me this priceless quote from Ralph Waldo Emerson: "One of life's illusions is that the present hour is not the critical decisive hour. Write it on your heart that each day is the best, the most crucial day in the year." To spend precious time in the grips of anxiety and worry is the ultimate travesty, when, as long as there is life, there is potential for the delight of love and meaningful achievement. Making the most of each priceless day is the ultimate challenge. We should begin each day in thoughtfulness of how we can make that day special, that day beautiful and meaningful. So long as there is breath, we have the shining potential for the best that life can offer. As my dad would have said: We must always remind ourselves to go for the gusto!

Congratulate Yourself!

Giving yourself legitimate credit for your accomplishments is not an excess, it is a virtue. When, because of your initiative, well-meaning and conscious efforts, you have pushed the reasonable boundaries, you deserve to acknowledge this, at least to yourself. This is not the same thing as bragging or conceit. Indeed, I have found that the acclaim of others can be a fleeting, ephemeral thing. We cannot count on others to recognize what is the best in us -- only real friends (a priceless commodity) can discern this. If we don't recognize and acknowledge our good deeds and accomplishments on our own, internal scorecard, we do not appropriately support, encourage and validate our own high standards and values. So, don't hesitate to give yourself a pat on the back for your achievements!

Count Your Blessings and Give Thanks

According to clinical research, feeling and expressing gratitude for the many priceless gifts of living is a positive attribute that augments personal well-being and facilitates personal sense of worth. It is a virtue to give thanks and show appreciation. Don't be stingy with your compliments or your gratitude. A worthwhile corollary to the notion of giving thanks and expressing gratitude is to always be cognizant that things could be much worse. Don't keep score of how you're doing by measuring material goods. Henry David Thoreau once said: "He is richest, whose pleasures are the cheapest."

Further Thoughts

Now that we are near the end of our discussion, my greatest hope is that you have been touched in some fashion or another with the ideas we have shared throughout these pages. My concept has always been that you will take the Protocol exercises and make them your own by inserting prompts and phrases that underscore what is most relevant for you. The exercises are intended to be done daily for as long as necessary, to anchor and imprint the desired results. When you have done all the work that is required to overcome your fear of cancer, you may choose to make your own recordings to address other issues in your life that may benefit from this kind of focused attention. Indeed, as I have stated before, I believe that, for everyone, mental exercise is just as important and beneficial as physical exercise. I encourage you to make it a regular part of your daily life.

There is one last script in the Protocol series of exercises that I propose may help you go even further towards developing those positive, optimistic qualities that have been the subject of our discussion. Put simply, we will create an exercise that encourages you to have confidence in the process and will reinforce your sense of optimism and positive expectancy for the future.

Chapter Fifteen

Increasing Confidence - Protocol Script 5

> *"The man who has no imagination has no wings."*
>
> -Mohammed Ali

In this last exercise, after first relaxing in a safe place, we will imagine what it would be like to have even more confidence in our bright future. I refer to this notion of increasing a desired response as "kicking it up a notch." Recall that, in our last exercise on "Optimistic Future Visualization," we worked on cultivating thoughts and images that supported, and were consistent with, our optimistic hopes and aspirations for the future. Once we were able to capture the body felt sensation of all that concept connotes, i.e. a secure, confident and pleasurable future, we worked to dial in that body felt sensation and to be able to recall it and come back to it. The logic here is that, even though our guided visualization has prompted a temporary response, we seek to reinforce that response by repeating the exercise as often as necessary until the desired results are "anchored" or "imprinted" on a permanent basis.

Protocol Script Five – Text with Explanation

Although the next exercise is similar in intent, it focuses primarily on augmenting or increasing our awareness of the pleasant body felt sensation that we seek. As with all the Protocol recordings, you may wish to be led into this exercise by an introduction involving Phase 2, "Relaxation and Finding a Safe Place" which has been reproduced below.

Protocol Script 5:
"Increasing Confidence – Kicking It Up a Notch," Text with Explanation

Increasing Confidence – Kicking It Up a Notch (with Explanation)

-Let yourself relax in a safe comfortable spot...

> *The first three steps in this exercise are designed to encourage muscle relaxation, which facilitates a stress-free, receptive state of mind.*

-It is okay if you are sitting, or if you are lying down...

-So long as you are comfortable and relaxed...

-Now focus your attention on your breathing...

> *You begin focusing on your breathing to access the relaxation response aspect of the autonomic nervous system. Realize, also, that you are channeling your awareness to your present breathing and away from an obsessive fear of cancer.*

-Take a deep breath and notice fresh oxygen entering your body...

-and when you exhale, feel the release of tension and stress...

-and as you are focusing on your breathing --

-notice how your abdomen rises and falls with each breath...

-Just breathe in calmness and relaxation...

-while you exhale tension and stress...

> *The above deep breathing routine can be repeated as many times as you wish until you feel the peaceful, calming relaxation response manifest in your body.*

-just gently turn your focus back to your breathing…

-and breathe in calmness and relaxation…

-while you exhale tension and stress…

-When you are ready, picture yourself somewhere that is safe and beautiful…

> *This is a deviation from strict mindfulness meditation, which remains passive throughout the process. Here, we are injecting a visualization that is designed to calm tension and reduce the stress of an anxious, worried mind that is preoccupied with the fear of cancer.*

-It can be a place where you have experienced contentment and joy in the past --

-or it can be a place that you make up in your imagination…

-Just let yourself daydream that you are in this safe and beautiful place…

> *You may have more than one safe place that comes to mind. There are no rules. Just choose the one that feels right and comes to you most clearly at this moment.*

-Notice how comfortable your body feels in this special place…

> *Because your stressful, anxious emotions are stored in your body, often at an unconscious level, all of our exercises will encourage you to be more aware of how you feel in your body. This can be surprisingly difficult to articulate.*

Later, when we focus on your fear of cancer, you will imagine what it would feel like to be rid of your anxiety and stress as a first step to overcoming them. For now, just enjoy the comfortable body sensation of being in your own favorite safe place.

-Notice any pleasing aromas, sights, or sounds…

The more you can use your senses to enhance a visualization, the more effectively it can influence communication with your reptilian and limbic brains, which do not respond to language but, rather, respond to vivid imagery.

-How do these pleasing aromas, sights or sounds make you feel in your body…

See if you can notice how specific stimuli create different body felt sensations.

-Is there music playing…

See if you can notice how specific stimuli create different body felt sensations.

-Is the sun shining in your special place…

See if you can notice how specific stimuli create different body felt sensations.

-Is it daytime or nighttime?

-Is anybody there with you in your special place?

-Notice how happy and relaxed you are in this safe and beautiful place...

-Notice the calmness and relaxation in your body

-and if other thoughts crowd your mind that is okay...

> *It is inevitable that your mind will drift. When this happens, just bring your focus back to your breathing and, when you are ready, resume the exercise where you left off.*

-just gently turn your focus back to your breathing

-and with each breath, inhale calmness and relaxation

-and exhale tension and stress

-Take some time to enjoy and explore this safe and beautiful spot

-Breath in calmness and relaxation --

-and exhale tension and stress

-Notice how this calmness and relaxation feels in your body

-Let go of whatever may be bothering you in the moment

> *This is an opportunity to go even deeper into relaxation -- to "put your worry on a shelf, alongside, and separate from you."*

-Just release the tension and stress

-and welcome the calmness and relaxation

-Give thanks for this special place where you can relax and be safe

> *Learning to appreciate and give thanks is a fundamental aspect of "savoring," which, as we shall see later, is a cornerstone of the Cancer as an Opportunity Protocol.*

-and realize that you can always return to this special place

-Whenever you want, you can experience this peace and relaxation

-Now savor this feeling in your body

-Take time to notice how your body feels in this safe place

-and realize that you can always come back—

-You will always be welcome here.

End of "Relaxation and Finding a Safe Place" introductory script. Continue with the "Increasing Confidence" script which follows.

[Note: After establishing your relaxation in a safe place, you are ready to probe your feelings regarding an optimistic future visualization which you developed in the previous Protocol scrip (number four)t. Here again, you will be asked to create your own script, based on your own personal experience and expectations. However, you may observe the following guidelines and customize them to fit your set of circumstances and expectations.]

Recall your daydream where you pictured your future life with more special, pleasurable experiences like the ones you have savored in the past…

And if one pleasant experience stands out, then see if you can locate where you experience this pleasant sensation in your body…

And notice, as much as possible, where you are, what you are doing and who is around you…

And, without stressing or straining, see if you can locate in your body where this pleasant feeling is located…

Can you picture this delightful feeling seeping into every cell in your body…?

Imagine that this wonderful feeling projects a soft, warm, invisible light all around you…

And that, although other people cannot see this light, they can feel its pleasant aura…

And, being in your safe place, comfortable and relaxed, see if you can daydream about having a similar pleasurable experience in the future one year, three years, or five years down the road…

Take some time to notice the details of what this feels like in your body…

Notice if you can identify a feeling of confidence that you can feel this way all the time…

Where is that feeling located in your body… Is it stronger in any one particular area… Where is it centered…

As you are enjoying this body felt sensation, can you picture what your posture is like, how you are standing in this special place…

What expression is on your face, are you smiling, are you speaking, what does this feel like in your face…

If you are speaking, how does your voice sound... Is it soft, or strong, are you laughing...

And notice that you are breathing in calmness and exhaling tension...

And how relaxed and comfortable you are in this safe place...

Can you dial up the body felt sensation of your sense of confidence in the future...

Can you imagine that there is a knob or dial on each cell that allows you to increase the quantity of your body felt sensation...

Take time to see if you can kick this whole thing up a notch...

While you are comfortable and relaxed, notice that your delightful body felt sensation is overflowing and radiating outward from your body and energizing anyone that may be around you...

What does this feel like in your body...

Could you feel this way all the time...

Take time to become familiar with the feel of this changed space in your body so that you can come back to it in the future...

Can you celebrate the sensual pleasure of this body felt sensation...

Can you give thanks for the safe place you have created and the unlimited opportunity for pleasure that you have been blessed with...

Can you give thanks for the time you have left in this life…

Can you practice living one day at a time -- making each day the best…

Can you savor this feeling in your body…

Take time to become familiar with the feel of this changed space in your body, so that you can come back to it in the future…

And realize that you can always come back…

And that you will always be welcome here…

And when you're ready, you can gently bring your attention back to the outer world…

But you can take with you to the outer world your body felt sense of peace and calm that is available to you in this special place inside you…

And as you return to the outer world, give thanks for this ability to go inside.

Bottom Line

Regardless of your prognosis, it is not necessary to convince yourself that your cancer will be just a "bump on the road," or that you will inevitably overcome the physical affliction of cancer. This may, or may not, be your destiny. There is no need to speculate or struggle to conjure up results that may be contradicted by the facts of your particular situation. Simply recognize that, regardless of ultimate outcome, it makes great sense to make the most of each precious day we are given. We basically do not know, nor can we predict, what lies ahead regarding our future health. Our challenge is to make the best memories we can today, regardless of whether the future offers perilous trials or, hopefully, smooth sailing ahead. The goal should be to create meaningful memories and peak experiences with whatever time we have.

It seems to me that if my health, and the healthy life to which I am accustomed, would become permanently impaired, I would be left with the challenge of savoring the good that life still offers regardless of impairment. If, for example, I were given 3 months to live, the best use of my time would be to savor my peak experiences from the past with which I have been blessed; give unfettered thanks; and spend the rest of my time saying goodbye to those whom I love and admire and celebrating our experience. Always accentuate the positive and, while acknowledging negative feelings, put them on the shelf, away from your core, so as not to let worry taint whatever precious time you may have left. I would like to check out of this life on a note of pure, unadulterated gratitude for the many blessings which I have been privileged to receive. I wish to avoid self-pity and acrimony. It is a wise man -- and in my book, a superhero -- who, in the face of death, can give thanks, smile, and celebrate the blessings that have been, without remorse and without reservation. May we all prove to be such superheroes.

Thank you for allowing me to share these very personal concepts with you. I am sending love and understanding as well as my fondest wishes that you will live your life in a manner that brings you the greatest joy, adventure and happiness. If you have any thoughts or ideas that you would like to share, please contact me. I appreciate your kind attention and wish you all the best.

Epilogue

There is a unique challenge in writing this book's epilogue where the author wishes to point out the dichotomy between the implications of a cancer death prognosis, when cancer is terminal, in contrast to the previous material in this book which has been written very much from the perspective of the cancer patient who is likely to survive.

In Cancer As An Opportunity, the focus is on neuro behavioral psychology and its application to guided visualization as a powerful mechanism to foster a therapeutic mindset that ameliorates the negative, pervasive and, ultimately, unhealthy mental accoutrements of cancer, worry and fear. The author's original discussion was focused more toward those cancer patients whose cancer can be cured, while attempting, hopefully, to integrate valuable insight for optimizing the cancer experience in any context. Ironically, he now finds himself engulfed with Stage 4 metastatic cancer that is not curable. Previous visualizations found in this book, where the patient emerges cancer free, are not entirely apropos to this epilogue discussion. However, I will attempt to share deeper and more profound truisms that have revealed themselves in my present situation.

The power of a positive and constructive attitude is a gift that can be applied to lift the soul by its bootstraps. This is not quite as obvious when the cancer patient has a limited time horizon and is constrained by fear of what lies beyond. In my own situation, after surviving a bout of prostate cancer (my post prostatectomy PSA was zero), two years later I was the victim of a devastating "widow maker" heart attack that led to an even more formidable diagnosis -- Stage IV metastatic adenocarcinoma that is not treatable.

The terminal cancer patient must first contend with the stark inevitability of their own mortality which, more than likely, must be faced sooner rather than later. Depending on the individual's life-after-death convictions, this mental confrontation can be resolved catastrophically - with manifold consternation – or, on the other hand, with consummate peace and calmness. In my own situation, not having been brought up with a religious background, I became jealous of my colleagues who were grounded with their faith in God. The core of their belief seemed to anchor them to positive outcomes that I could only imagine. Always a pragmatist, I observed that those who were comforted by their belief in God dealt with the ultimate challenge of end-of-life with a much more positive and spiritual outlook. I reasoned that to believe in a wholesome and constructive life after death could not hurt: if my interpretation of things was correct, I should be rewarded with the blessings that are alluded to in the spiritual writings. On the other hand, if my positive ruminations are ill-founded then my fate should be no worse than the majority of those who do not believe in a life after death based on beauty and grace.

Consider the words of Psalm 16, which were provided to me by a well-meaning colleague:

> *Thou wilt show me the path of life:*
>
> *In thy presence is fullness of joy;*
>
> *at thy right-hand there are pleasures for evermore.*

Certainly, my life has been colored with a copious share of joy and fullness. In this time of death contemplation, I am overwhelmingly drawn by the notion of the "pleasures for evermore" at my right hand, as the Psalm promises. Shortly after my massive heart attack, I was far from a decent model of positivity; on the contrary, I was besieged with doubt, grief and bitterness at the notion of the termination of my heretofore happy and successful existence on planet Earth. My heart ached at the notion of projects unfinished and delightful interludes that would never materialize. However, surrounded by my sweet, ever loving wife and my three gracious daughters, my thoughts found themselves ever lured by the contemplation of the joyous fulfillment that had previously exemplified my human experience. The notion, as in Psalm 16, of "pleasures evermore,' guided my reflection to a sweet and enticing, peaceful shore. I decided to spend the rest of my days on earth celebrating the blessed experiences that had bathed my earthly life with love.

As I write this epilogue, I do not know how much time I have left in this world. But that is a fact that we all must contemplate – cancer diagnosis or not. My desire for you, the reader, is that this book will be a source of worthwhile techniques (and, perhaps, a healthy dose of inspiration!) to maximize the enjoyment and appreciation of your life regardless of your physical health.

Thomas Myers
May 2019

Thomas Myers passed away on May 21, 2019.

He did, indeed, maximize the enjoyment and appreciation of his life even during his final battle with cancer.

References

1. Achterberg J. Psychological factors and blood chemistries as disease outcome predictors for cancer patients. Multivariate Exper Clin Res 1977;3:107-122.
2. Adamsen, L., Midtgaard, J., Rorth, M., Borregaard, N., Andersen, C., Quist, M., et al. Feasibility, physical capacity, and health benefits of a multidimensional exercise program for cancer patients undergoing chemotherapy. Supportive Care in Cancer. 2003;11:707–716.
3. Adler, M.G., & Fagley, N.S. (2005). Appreciation: Individual differences in finding value and meaning as a unique predictor of subjective well-being, Journal of Personality, 73, 79-114.
4. Ahles, T.A., Tope, D.M., Pinkson, B., Walch, S., Hann, D., Whedon, M., et al. Massage therapy for patients undergoing autologous bone marrow transplantation. Journal of Pain and Symptom Management. 1999;18:157–163.
5. Ali, N.S., Khalil, H.Z. Effect of psychoeducational intervention on anxiety among Egyptian bladder cancer patients. Cancer Nursing. 1989;12:236–242.
6. Allison, P.J., Nicolau, B., Edgar, L., Archer, J., Black, M., Hier, M. Teaching head and neck cancer patients coping strategies: results of a feasibility study. Oral Oncology. 2004;40:538–544.
7. Ambler, N., Rumsey, N., Harcourt, D., Khan, F., Cawthorn, S., Barker, J. Specialist nurse counsellor interventions at the time of diagnosis of breast cancer: comparing 'advocacy' with a conventional approach. Journal of Advanced Nursing. 1999;29:445–453.
8. Andersen, B.L., Farrar, W.B., Golden-Kreutz, D.M., Glaser, R., Emery, C.F., Crespin, T.R., et al. Psychological, behavioral, and immune changes after a psychological

intervention: a clinical trial. Journal of Clinical Oncology. 2004;22:3570–3580.
9. Antoni, M.H., Lehman, J.M., Kilbourn, K.M., Boyers, A.E., Culver, J.L., Alferi, S.M., et al. Cognitive-behavioral stress management intervention decreases the prevalence of depression and enhances benefit finding among women under treatment for early-stage breast cancer. Health Psychology. 2001;20:20–32.
10. Arakawa, S. Relaxation to reduce nausea, vomiting, and anxiety induced by chemotherapy in Japanese patients. Cancer Nursing. 1997;20:342–349.
11. Arlow, J.A. (1990). Emotion, time, and the self. In R. Pluthik & H. Kellerman (Eds.), Emotion: Theory, research, and experience (Vol. 5, pp. 133-146). San Diecgo, CA: Academic Press.
12. Aronson, E. & Linder, D., (1965). Gain and loss of esteem as determinants of interpersonal attractiveness. Journal of Experimental Social Psychology, 1, 156-171.
13. Barnes, L.L.B, Harp, D., Jung, W.S. Reliability generalization of scores on the Spielberger State-Trait Anxiety Inventory. Educational and Psychological Measurement. 2002;62:603–618.
14. Berenbaum, H. (2002). Varieties of joy-related pleasurable activities and feelings. Cognition & Emotion, 16, 473-494.
15. Bieliauskas L., & Garron D. (1982) Psychological depression and cancer. General Hospital Psychiatry, 4, 187-195.
16. Bjelland, I., Dahl, A.A., Haug, T.T., Neckelmann, D. The validity of the Hospital Anxiety and Depression Scale. An updated literature review. Journal of Psychosomatic Research. 2002;52:69–77.
17. Boesen, E.H., Ross, L., Frederiksen, K., Thomsen, B.L., Dahlstrom, K., Schmidt, G., et al. Psychoeducational intervention for patients with cutaneous malignant melanoma:

A replication study. Journal of Clinical Oncology. 2005;23:1270–1277.
18. Borkovec, T.D. (1985). Worry: A potentially valuable concept. Behavior Research and Therapy, 23, 481-483.
19. Brandberg, Y., Bolund, C., Sigurdardottir, V., Sjoden, P.O., Sullivan, M. Anxiety and depressive symptoms at different stages of malignant melanoma. Psycho-Oncology. 1992;1:71–78.
20. Brown, K.W., & Ryan, R.M. (2003). The benefits of being present: Mindfulness and its role in psychological well-being. Journal of Personality and Social Psychology, 84, 822-848.
21. Bryant, F.B. & Cvengros, J.A. (2004). Distinguishing hope and optimism: Two sides of a coin, or two separate coins? Journal of Social and Clinical Psychology, 23, 273-302.
22. Bryant, F.B. (2003). Savoring Beliefs Inventory (SBI): A scale for measuring beliefs about savoring, Journal of Mental Health, 12, 175-196.
23. Bryant, F.B., Smart, C.M. & King, S.P. (2005). Using the past to enhance the present: Boosting happiness through positive reminiscence. Journal of Happiness Studies,6, 227-260.
24. Bryk, A.S., Raudenbush, S.W. Hierarchical linear models: Applications and data analysis methods. Thousand Oaks, CA: Sage Publications; 1992.
25. Bultz, B.D., Johansen, C. Screening for distress, the 6th vital sign: Where are we, and where are we going? Psycho-Oncology. 2011; 20(6): 569-571.
26. Burton, M.V., Parker, R.W. A randomized control trial of preoperative psychology preparation for mastectomy. Psycho-Oncology. 1995;4:1–19.
27. Campbell, D.T., Kenny, D.A. A primer on regression artifacts. New York, NY: Guilford Press; 1999.
28. Campbell, M.K., Tessaro, I., Gellin, M., et al. Adult cancer survivorship care: experiences from the LIVESTRONG

centers of excellence network. Journal of Cancer Survivorship. 2011; 5(3): 271-282. doi: 10.1007/s11764-011-0180-z
29. Carey, M.P., Burish, T.G. Anxiety as a predictor of behavioral therapy outcome for cancer chemotherapy patients. Journal of Consulting and Clinical Psychology. 1985;53:860–865.
30. Carlson, L.E., Bultz, B.D. Cancer distress screening. Needs, models, and methods. Journal of Psychosomatic Research. 2003;55:403–409.
31. Carmack Taylor, C.L., de Moor, C., Basen-Engquist, K., Smith, M.A., Dunn, A.L., Badr, H., et al. Moderator analyses of participants in the Active for Life after cancer trial: implications for physical activity group intervention studies. Annals of Behavioral Medicine. 2007;33:99–104.
32. Cartledge Hoff, A., Haaga, D.A.F. Effects of an education program on radiation oncology patients and families. Journal of Psychosocial Oncology. 2005;23:61–79.
33. Carty, J.L. Dissertation Abstracts International. Vol. 51. 1990. Relaxation with imagery: An adjunctive treatment for anticipatory nausea and/or vomiting (Doctoral dissertation, The Catholic University of America, 1990) p. 131.
34. Cheung, Y.L., Molassiotis, A., Chang, A.M. The effect of progressive muscle relaxation training on anxiety and quality of life after stoma surgery in colorectal cancer patients. Psycho-Oncology. 2003;12:254–266.
35. Cohen, L., Warneke, C., Fouladi, R.T., Rodriguez, M.A., Chaoul-Reich, A. Psychological adjustment and sleep quality in a randomized trial of the effects of a Tibetan yoga intervention in patients with lymphoma. Cancer. 2004;100:2253–2260.
36. Comer, J. Interfact between research and practice in psycho-oncology. Acta Oncologica. 1999; 38:703-707.
37. Compas, B.E., Haaga, D.A., Keefe, F., et al. Sampling of empirically supported psychological treatments from health psychology: smoking, chronic pain, cancer, and bulimia

nervosa. Journal of Consulting and Clinical Psychology 1998; 66(1): 89-112.
38. Coyne, J.C., Lepore, S.J., Palmer, S.C. Efficacy of psychosocial interventions in cancer care: evidence is weaker than it first looks. Annals of Behavioral Medicine. 2006;32:104–110.
39. Crawford, J.R., Henry, J.D., Crombie, C., Taylor, E.P. Normative data for the HADS from a large non-clinical sample. British Journal of Clinical Psychology. 2001;40:429–434.
40. Cull, A., Stewart, M., Altman, D.G. Assessment of and intervention for psychosocial problems in routine oncology practice. British Journal of Cancer. 1995;72:229–235.
41. Davidson, J.R., Waisberg, J.L., Brundage, M.D., MacLean, A.W. Nonpharmacologic group treatment of insomnia: a preliminary study with cancer survivors. Psycho-Oncology. 2001;10:389–397.
42. Davison, B.J., Degner, L.F. Empowerment of men newly diagnosed with prostate cancer. Cancer Nursing. 1997;20:187–196.
43. Derogotis, L.R., Morrow, G.R., Fetting, J., et al. (1983). The prevalence of psychiatric disorders among cancer patients. Journal of the American Medical Assoc. 1983; 249(6):751-757.
44. Deshields, T.L., Nanna, S.K. Providing care for the "whole patient" in the cancer setting: The psycho-oncology consultation model of patient care. Journal of Clinical Psychology in Med Setting. 2010; 17:249-257.
45. Deshields, T.L., Nanna, S.K. Providing care for the "whole patient" in the cancer setting: The psycho-oncology consultation model of patient care. Journal of Clinical Psychology in Med Setting. 2010; 17:249-257.
46. Diener, E., Sandvik, E., & Pavot, W. (1991). Happiness is the frequency, not the intensity, of positive versus negative affect.

In F. Strack, M. Argyle, & N. Schwarz (Eds.), Subjective well-being: An interdisciplinary perspective (pp. 119-139). New York: Pergamon.
47. Division of Cancer Control & Population Sciences, National Cancer Institute, U.S. National Institutes of Health. (2011). Cancer control framework and synthesis rationale. Available at: http://cancercontrol.cancer.gov/od/about.html. Last accessed May 2013.
48. Dobkin, P.L. Dissertation Abstracts International. Vol. 48. 1987. The use of systematic desensitization, a biobehavioral intervention, in the reduction of aversive chemotherapy side effects in cancer patients (Doctoral dissertation, University of Georgia, 1987) p. 163.
49. Dodd, M.J. Efficacy of proactive information on self-care in chemotherapy patients. Patient Education and Counseling. 1988;11:215–225.
50. Dodd, M.J. Efficacy of proactive information on self-care in radiation therapy patients. Heart & Lung. 1987;16:538–544.
51. Dohan, D., Schrag, D. Using navigators to improve care of underserved patients. Cancer. 2005;104(4):848-855.
52. Doorenbos, A., Given, B., Given, C., Verbitsky, N. Physical functioning: effect of behavioral intervention for symptoms among individuals with cancer. Nursing Research. 2006;55:161–171.
53. Duckworth, A.L., Steen, T.A., & Seligman, M.E.P. (2005). Positive psychology in clinical practice. Annual Review of Clinical Psychology, 1, 629-651.
54. Duclos, S.E., Laird, J.D., Schneider, F., Sexter, M., Stern, L., & Van Lighten, O. (1989). Emotion-specific effects of facial expressions and postures on emotional experience. Journal of Personality and Social Psychology, 57, 100-108.
55. Ellwood, A.L, Carlson, L.E, Bultz, B.D. Empirically supported treatments: will this movement in the field of

psychology impact the practice of psychosocial oncology? Psycho-Oncology. 2001; 10(3): 199-205.
56. Elsesser, K., Van Berkel, M., Sartory, G., Biermann-Göcke, W., et al. The effects of anxiety management training on psychological variables and immune parameters in cancer patients: A pilot study. Behavioural & Cognitive Psychotherapy. 1994;22:13–23.
57. Erber, R., Wegner, D.M., & Therriault, N. (1996). On being cool and collected: Mood regulation in anticipation of social interaction. Journal of Personality and Social Psychology, 70,757-766.
58. Evans, D.I., McCartney, C.F., & Nemeroff, C.N., et al (1986). Depression in women treated for gynecological cancer: clinical and neuroendocrine assessment. American Journal of Psychiatry 1986; 143:447-452.
59. Feldman, C.S. Dissertation Abstracts International. Vol. 50. 1989. The role of imagery in the hypnotic treatment of adverse reactions to cancer chemotherapy (Doctoral dissertation, University of South Carolina, 1989) pp. 4216–4217.
60. Finney, J.W. Regression to the mean in substance use disorder treatment research. Addiction. 2008;103:42–52.
61. Fox B. Issues in research on premorbid psychological factors and cancer incidence. Cancer Detection & Prevention 1979; 2(2):257-259.
62. Fukui, S., Kugaya, A., Okamura, H., Kamiya, M., Koike, M., Nakanishi, T., et al. A psychosocial group intervention for Japanese women with primary breast carcinoma. Cancer. 2000;89:1026–1036.
63. Furukawa, T.A., Barbui, C., Cipriani, A., Brambilla, P., Watanabe, N. Imputing missing standard deviations in meta-analyses can provide accurate results. Journal of Clinical Epidemiology. 2006;59:7–10.
64. Gaston-Johansson, F., Fall-Dickson, J.M., Nanda, J., Ohly, K.V., Stillman, S., Krumm, S., et al. The effectiveness of the

comprehensive coping strategy program on clinical outcomes in breast cancer autologous bone marrow transplantation. Cancer Nursing. 2000;23:277–285.
65. Gendlin E.T., (1981). Focusing. New York: Bantam Books.
66. Gendlin E.T., McGuire, M., & Grindler, D. (1984). Imagery, body and space in focusing. In: Sheikh AA, editor. Imagination and healing. New York: Baywood Publishing Co., p. 276-286.
67. Gendlin, E.T. (1969). Focusing. Psychotherapy: Theory, Research, and Practice, 6:4-14.
68. Given, C., Given, B., Rahbar, M., Jeon, S., McCorkle, R., Cimprich, B., et al. Effect of a cognitive behavioral intervention on reducing symptom severity during chemotherapy. Journal of Clinical Oncology. 2004;22:507–516.
69. Goodwin, P.J., Leszcz, M., Ennis, M., Koopmans, J., Vincent, L., Guther, H., et al. The effect of group psychosocial support on survival in metastatic breast cancer. New England Journal of Medicine. 2001;345:1719–1726.
70. Greer, S., Moorey, S., Baruch, J. Evaluation of adjuvant psychological therapy for clinically referred cancer patients. British Journal of Cancer. 1991;63:257–260.
71. Greer, S., Moorey, S., Baruch, J.D., Watson, M., Robertson, B.M., Mason, A., et al. Adjuvant psychological therapy for patients with cancer: a prospective randomised trial. The BMJ. 1992;304:675–680.
72. Hagopian, G.A., Rubenstein, J.H. Effects of telephone call interventions on patients' well-being in a radiation therapy department. Cancer Nursing. 1990;13:339–344.
73. Hamann, S.B., Ely, T.D., Hoffman, J.M., & Kilts, C.D. (2002). Ecstasy and agony: Activation of the human amygdala in positive and negative emotion. Psychological Science, 13, 135-141.

74. Harrison, J., Maguire, P. Predictors of psychiatric morbidity in cancer patients. British Journal of Psychiatry. 1994;165:593–598.
75. Harrop, J.P., Dean, J.A., Paskett, E.D. Cancer Survivorship Research: A Review of the Literature and Summary of Current NCI-Designated Cancer Center Projects. Cancer Epidemiology Biomarkers and Prevention. 2011; 20(10): 2042-2047.
76. Helgeson, V.S., Lepore, S.J., Eton DT. Moderators of the benefits of psychoeducational interventions for men with prostate cancer. Health Psychology. 2006;25:348–354.
77. Hidderley, M., Holt, M. A pilot randomized trial assessing the effects of autogenic training in early stage cancer patients in relation to psychological status and immune system responses. European Journal of Oncology Nursing. 2004;8:61–65.
78. Higgins, J.P., Thompson, S.G., Deeks, J.J., Altman, D.G. Measuring inconsistency in meta-analyses. BMJ. 2003;327:557–560.
79. Holland, J.C. Psychological Care of Patients: Psycho-Oncology's Contribution. Journal of Clinical Oncology, 2003; 21 90230): 253s-265.
80. Holland, J.C., Weiss, T.R. History of psycho-oncology. Psycho-Oncology. 2010. Oxford University Press.
81. Hosaka, T., Sugiyama, Y., Tokuda, Y., Okuyama, T. Persistent effects of a structured psychiatric intervention on breast cancer patients' emotions. Psychiatry and Clinical Neurosciences. 2000;54:559–563.
82. Institute of Medicine. (2008). Cancer Care for the Whole Patient: Meeting psychosocial health needs. In N. E. Adler & A. E. K. Page (Eds.). Washington, DC: Institution of Medicine.
83. Jacobsen, P.B. Promoting evidence-based psychosocial care for cancer patients. Psycho-Oncology. 2009; 18(1): 6-13.

84. Jacobsen, P.B. Screening for psychological distress in cancer patients: challenges and opportunities. Journal of Clinical Oncology. 2007;25:4526–4527.
85. Jacobsen, P.B., Donovan, K.A., Trask, P.C., et al. Screening for psychologic distress in ambulatory cancer patients. Cancer. 2005;103(7):1494-1502.
86. Jacobsen, P.B., Jim, H.S. Psychosocial interventions for anxiety and depression in adult cancer patients: achievements and challenges. CA Cancer Journal for Clinicians. 2008; 58(4): 214-230. doi: CA.2008.0003 [pii]10.3322/CA.2008.0003
87. Jensen, M. (1987). Psychobiological factors predicting the course of breast cancer. Journal of Personality, 55, pp. 317-342.
88. Kalaian HA, Raudenbush SW. A multivariate mixed linear model for meta-analysis. Psychological Methods. 1996;1:227–235.
89. Kanter, M. (1982-1983). Clearing a space with four cancer patients. Focusing Folio, 2(4), 23-36.
90. Keller M, Sommerfeldt S, Fischer C, Knight L, Riesbeck M, Lowe B, et al. Recognition of distress and psychiatric morbidity in cancer patients: a multi-method approach. Annals of Oncology. 2004;15:1243–1249.
91. Kendall, J., Glaze, K., Oakland, S., et al. What do 1281 distress screeners tell us about cancer patients in a community cancer center? Psycho-Oncology. 2011;20(6): 594-600.
92. Kim SD, Kim HS. Effects of a relaxation breathing exercise on anxiety, depression, and leukocyte in hemopoietic stem cell transplantation patients. Cancer Nursing. 2005;28:79–83.
93. King AC, Ahn DF, Atienza AA, Kraemer HC. Exploring refinements in targeted behavioral medicine intervention to advance public health. Annals of Behavioral Medicine. 2008;35:251–260.

94. Kissane DW, Bloch S, Smith GC, Miach P, Clarke DM, Ikin J, et al. Cognitive-existential group psychotherapy for women with primary breast cancer: a randomised controlled trial. Psycho-Oncology. 2003;12:532–546.
95. Kissane DW, Grabsch B, Clarke DM, Smith GC, Love AW, Bloch S, et al. Supportive-expressive group therapy for women with metastatic breast cancer: survival and psychosocial outcome from a randomized controlled trial. Psycho-Oncology. 2007;16:277–286.
96. Kite SM, Maher EJ, Anderson K, Young T, Young J, Wood J, et al. Development of an aromatherapy service at a Cancer Centre. Palliative Medicine. 1998;12:171–180.
97. Knight, S. Oncology and hematology. In P. Camic & S. Knight (Eds.), Clinical handbook of health psychology. 2004. Cambridge, MA: Hogrefe & Huber Publishers.
98. Kobasa S, Maddi S, & Courington S. Personality and constitution as mediators in the stress-illness relationship. Journal of Health & Social Behavior 1981;22:368-378.
99. Kwekkeboom KL. Music versus distraction for procedural pain and anxiety in patients with cancer. Oncology Nursing Forum. 2003;30:433–440.
100. Lepore SJ, Coyne JC. Psychological interventions for distress in cancer patients: a review of reviews. Annals of Behavioral Medicine. 2006;32:85–92.
101. Lin ML, Tsang YM, Hwang SL. Efficacy of a stress management program for patients with hepatocellular carcinoma receiving transcatheter arterial embolization. Journal of the Formosan Medical Association. 1998;97:113–117.
102. Lindemalm C, Strang P, Lekander M. Support group for cancer patients. Does it improve their physical and psychological wellbeing? A pilot study. Supportive Care in Cancer. 2005;13:652–657.

103. Liossi C, White P. Efficacy of clinical hypnosis in the enhancement of quality of life of terminally ill cancer patients. Contemporary Hypnosis. 2001;18:145–160.
104. Lipsey MW. Those confounded moderators in meta-analysis: Good, bad, and ugly. Annals of the American Academy of Political and Social Science. 2003;587:69–81.
105. Loscalzo, M.J., Butz, B.D., Jacobsen, P.B. Building psychosocial programs: a roadmap to excellence. In: Holland, JC, et al. eds. Psycho-Oncology. New York, NY: Oxford University Press; 2010:569-574.
106. Mantovani G, Astara G, Lampis B, Bianchi A, Curreli L, Orru W, et al. Evaluation by multidimensional instruments of health-related quality of life of elderly cancer patients undergoing three different psychosocial treatment approaches. A randomized clinical trial. Supportive Care in Cancer. 1996;4:129–140.
107. Massie, M.J., & Holland, J.C. (1990). Depression and the cancer patient. Journal of Clinical Psychiatry, 517 (Suppl July), pp.12-19.
108. McQuellon RP, Wells M, Hoffman S, Craven B, Russell G, Cruz J, et al. Reducing distress in cancer patients with an orientation program. Psycho-Oncology. 1998;7:207–217.
109. Meyer TJ, Mark MM. Effects of psychosocial interventions with adult cancer patients: a meta-analysis of randomized experiments. Health Psychology. 1995;14:101–108.
110. Midtgaard J, Rorth M, Stelter R, Tveteras A, Andersen C, Quist M, et al. The impact of a multidimensional exercise program on self-reported anxiety and depression in cancer patients undergoing chemotherapy: a phase II study. Palliative and Supportive Care. 2005;3:197–208.
111. Mitchell AJ. Pooled results from 38 analyses of the accuracy of distress thermometer and other ultra-short methods of detecting cancer-related mood disorders. Journal of Clinical Oncology. 2007;25:4670–4681.

112. Mitchell, A.J. Short screening tools for cancer-related distress: a review and diagnostic validity meta-qnalysis. Journal of National Comprehensive Cancer Network. 2010;8:487-494.
113. Miyashita M. A randomized intervention study for breast cancer survivors in Japan: effects of short-term support group focused on possible breast cancer recurrence. Cancer Nursing. 2005;28:70–78.
114. Montazeri A, Jarvandi S, Haghighat S, Vahdani M, Sajadian A, Ebrahimi M, et al. Anxiety and depression in breast cancer patients before and after participation in a cancer support group. Patient Education and Counseling. 2001;45:195–198.
115. Moorey S, Greer S, Bliss J, Law M. A comparison of adjuvant psychological therapy and supportive counselling in patients with cancer. Psycho-Oncology. 1998;7:218–228.
116. Morrow GR. Effect of the cognitive hierarchy in the systematic desensitization treatment of anticipatory nausea in cancer patients: A component comparison with relaxation only, counseling, and no treatment. Cognitive Therapy and Research. 1986;10:421–446.
117. Moyer A, Sohl SJ, Knapp-Oliver SK, Schneider S. Characteristics and methodological quality of 25 years of research investigating psychosocial interventions for cancer patients. Cancer Treatment Reviews. 2009;35:475–484.
118. Moynihan C, Bliss JM, Davidson J, Burchell L, Horwich A. Evaluation of adjuvant psychological therapy in patients with testicular cancer: randomised controlled trial. BMJ. 1998;316:429–435.
119. National Cancer Policy Board, Institute of Medicine. From cancer patient to cancer survivor: Lost in transition. 2005. Washington, D.C.:The National Academies Press.
120. National Comprehensive Cancer Network. (2009). Clinical Practice Guidelines in Oncology, Distress Management. 1. Available at: www.nccn.org. Last accessed May 2013.

121. National Comprehensive Cancer Network. NCCN clinical practice guidelines in oncology: distress management - v.1.2008. National Comprehensive Cancer Network; 2008.
122. Newell SA, Sanson-Fisher RW, Savolainen NJ. Systematic review of psychological therapies for cancer patients: overview and recommendations for future research. Journal of the National Cancer Institute. 2002;94:558–584.
123. Office of Cancer Centers, National Cancer Institute, National Institutes of Health. (2010) Policies and guidelines relating to the cancer center support grant. Available at: http://cancercenters.cancer.gov/documents/CCSG_Guidelines.pdf. Last accessed May 2013.
124. Osborne, R.H., Elsworth, G.R., Hopper, J.L. Age-specific norms and determinants of anxiety and depression in 731 women with breast cancer recruited through a population-based cancer registry. European Journal of Cancer. 2003;39:755–762.
125. Palekar, I.S. Dissertation Abstracts International. Vol. 56. 1994. Effect of autogenic relaxation with imagery on chemotherapy side effects, as predicted by personality characteristics (Doctoral dissertation, The University of Akron, 1994) p. 311.
126. Parry, C., Kent, E., Mariotto, A.B., Alfano, C.M., et al. Cancer survivors: a booming population. Cancer Epidemiology Biomarkers and Prevention. 2011; 20(10):1996-2005.
127. Poroch, D. The effect of preparatory patient education on the anxiety and satisfaction of cancer patients receiving radiation therapy. Cancer Nursing. 1995;18:206–214.
128. Powell, C.B., Kneier, A., Chen, et al. A randomized study of the effectiveness of a brief psychosocial intervention for women attending a gynecologic cancer clinic. Gynecologic Oncology. 2008; 111(1):137-143.

129. Reynolds, P., & Kaplan, G.A. (1990) Social Connections and risk for cancer: prospective evidence from the Alameda Country Study. Behavorial Medicine, 16L, 101-110.
130. Robison, L., Demark-Wahnefried, W. Cancer survivorship: focusing on future research opportunities. Cancer Epidemiology Biomarkers and Prevention. 2011; 20(10): 1994-1995.
131. Ryff, C. (1989). Happiness is everything, or is it? Explorations on the meaning of psychological well-being. Journal of Personality and Social Psychology, 57, 1069-1081.
132. Spiegel, D. (1993). Psychosocial intervention in cancer. Journal of National Cancer Institute, 85, 1198-1205.
133. Spiegel, D. (1994). Health caring: Psychosocial support for patients with cancer. Cancer, 74(Suppl.),1453-1457.
134. Spiegel, D., & Sands, S.H. (1989). Psychological influences on metastatic disease progression. In: Gorelik, E.L (ed). Metastasis/dissemination. Dordrecht, Netherlands: Kluwer.
135. Strack, F., Schwarz, N., & Gschneidinger, E. (1985). Happiness and reminiscing: The role of time perspective, affect, and mode of thinking. Journal of Personality and Social Psychology, 49, 1460-1469.
136. Tracy, J.L., & Robins, R.W. (2004). Show your pride: Evidence for a discrete emotion expression. Psychological Science, 15, 194-197.
137. Van Egeren, L. Assessment approaches in health psychology. In P. Camic & S. Knight (Eds.), Clinical handbook of health psychology. 2004. Cambridge, MA: Hogrefe & Huber Publishers.
138. Weibe DJ, Williams PG. Hardiness and health: a social psychophysiological perspective on stress and adaptation. Journal of Social & Clinical Psychology 1992;11:238-262.

Appendix A

Protocol Scripts 1 through 5

Protocol Script 1:
"Relaxing and Finding a Safe Place"

Relaxing and Finding a Safe Place

-Let yourself relax in a safe comfortable spot…

-It is okay if you are sitting, or if you are lying down…

-So long as you are comfortable and relaxed…

-Now focus your attention on your breathing…

-Take a deep breath and notice fresh oxygen entering your body…

-and when you exhale, feel the release of tension and stress…

-and as you are focusing on your breathing --

-notice how your abdomen rises and falls with each breath…

-Just breathe in calmness and relaxation…

-while you exhale tension and stress…

-and if other thoughts crowd your mind that is okay…

-just gently turn your focus back to your breathing…

-and breathe in calmness and relaxation…

-while you exhale tension and stress…

-When you are ready, picture yourself somewhere that is safe and beautiful…

-It can be a place where you have experienced contentment and joy in the past --

-or it can be a place that you make up in your imagination…

-Just let yourself daydream that you are in this safe and beautiful place…

-Notice how comfortable your body feels in this special place…

-Notice any pleasing aromas, sights, or sounds…

-How do these pleasing aromas, sights or sounds make you feel in your body…

-Is there music playing…

-Is the sun shining in your special place…

-Is it daytime or nighttime?

-Is anybody there with you in your special place?

-Notice how happy and relaxed you are in this safe and beautiful place…

-Notice the calmness and relaxation in your body…

-and if other thoughts crowd your mind, that is okay…

-just gently turn your focus back to your breathing…

-and with each breath, inhale calmness and relaxation…

-and exhale tension and stress…

-Take some time to enjoy and explore this safe and beautiful spot…

-Breath in calmness and relaxation --

-and exhale tension and stress…

-Notice how this calmness and relaxation feels in your body…

-Let go of whatever may be bothering you in the moment...

-Just release the tension and stress...

-and welcome the calmness and relaxation...

-Give thanks for this special place where you can relax and be safe...

-and realize that you can always return to this special place...

-Whenever you want, you can experience this peace and relaxation...

-Now savor this feeling in your body...

-Take time to notice how your body feels in this safe place...

-and realize that you can always come back—

-You will always be welcome here...

-When you are ready, you can gently bring your attention back to the outer world...

-But you can take with you to the outer world your body felt sense of peace and calm...

-that is available to you in this special place inside you...

-As you return to the outer world, give thanks for this ability to go inside.

End of "Relaxing and Finding a Safe Place"

Notes:

Protocol Script 2:
"Relaxation and Making Friends with your Fear"

Relaxation and Making Friends with your Fear

-Ask yourself, "How am I feeling right now?" Let your body do the answering…

-Ask yourself, "How does realizing that I have cancer, feel in my body?"…

-Ask yourself, "Where do I feel this fear of cancer in my body?"…

-Ask yourself, "In what ways does my fear of cancer stand between me and being really happy?" Let your body do the answering.…

-Is it okay to be with how all this feels, right now? …

-Ask yourself: "How does the worst of this feel inside my body?

-If this feeling is so overwhelming, that you want to run away from it, then take some time to create an atmosphere of warmth and caring acceptance…

-See if you can treat this hurting place inside with gentleness and kindness in a way that it can feel that presence from you…

-Can you create a feeling climate towards this body felt sensation that is the opposite of the way you usually treat it…

-Is it possible to hold this feeling in your body in the same way you might hold and nurture a hurting child? …

-Can you imagine putting your arm around this place in your body and patting it, or stroking it? …

-Notice where you feel this fear most in your body and place your hand there to comfort, pat and caress it, or just let it know from your touch that you care and that you are present....

-Can you do your best to become friends with, and accept, your fear?

-Now ask yourself, what needs to change inside of me for this whole thing to begin to feel better...

-What would feel like a small step forward with all this...

-What would feel like a breath of fresh air in this whole thing...

-Imagine for a moment, how it would feel inside if this whole thing were all okay...

-Could you feel this way all the time...?

-Take time to become familiar with the feel of this changed space in your body so that you can come back to it in the future...

End of "Relaxation and Making Friends with your Fear"

Notes:

Protocol Script 3:
"Positive Reflection (Reverie)"

Positive Reflection (Reverie)

-As you relax in a safe place let your mind recall how you felt before you were diagnosed with cancer…

-How did that feel in your body…

-Can you remember any past special experiences, special times and special events that you recall with particular joy?

-What was enjoyable about that special event…

-How did that feel in your body…

-Where did you feel that enjoyable sensation in your body…

-Imagine how you would act if you were there at your special event: What would you be doing… What would you be saying…

-Imagine the facial expressions you would have if you were there at your special event…

-Imagine the sounds you would hear, if you were there at your special event…

-What does all this feel like in your body…

-Can you isolate the body felt sensation of that experience and dial it up a notch…

-Can you remember any past special experiences, special times and special events that you recall with special personal pride over your accomplishments?

-What was enjoyable or rewarding about that special event…

-Where did you feel that enjoyable sensation in your body...

-Imagine how you would act if you were there at your special event: What would you be doing... What would you be saying...

-Imagine the facial expressions you would have if you were there at your special event...

-Imagine the sounds you would hear, if you were there at your special event...

-What does all this feel like in your body...

-Can you isolate the body felt sensation of that experience and dial it up a notch...

-Can you remember any past special experiences, special times and special events that you recall with warm feelings of friendship or love?

-What was enjoyable about that special event...

-How did that feel in your body...

-Where did you feel that enjoyable sensation in your body...

-Imagine how you would act if you were there at your special event: What would you be doing... What would you be saying...

-Imagine the facial expressions you would have if you were there at your special event...

-Imagine the sounds you would hear, if you were there at your special event...

-What does all this feel like in your body...

-Can you isolate the body felt sensation of that experience and dial it up a notch…

-Can you give thanks for these special experiences…

-and realize that you will always have these memories and special occasions to remind you of just how good life can be…

-and that you can always return to this special place…

-Whenever you want, you can experience this peace and relaxation…

-Now savor this feeling in your body…

-Take time to notice how your body feels in this safe place and these beautiful memories…

-and realize that you can always come back—

-You will always be welcome here.

End of "Positive Reflection (Reverie)"

Notes:

Protocol Script 4:
"Optimistic Future Visualization"

"Optimistic Future Visualization"

-Can you picture your future life with more special, pleasurable experiences like the ones you have just savored in Protocol Script 3, "Positive Past Reflection (Reverie)"...

-Just take your time and sort through your previous special, pleasurable experiences...

-Take all the time you want to savor and enjoy these past pleasurable experiences...

-And if you have more than one pleasurable experience, just choose the experience that seems to have the most energy for you, right now...

-And if one pleasant experience stands out, then see if you can locate where you experience this pleasant sensation in your body...

-Just relax, enjoy, and savor this experience as much as you like...

-Can you picture this delightful feeling seeping pleasantly into every cell in your body...

-Imagine that this wonderful feeling projects a soft, warm, invisible light all around you...

-Imagine that other people cannot see this light, but that they can feel its pleasant aura...

-Now realize you are still in your safe place, breathing in calmness and exhaling tension...

-And, being in your safe place, comfortable and relaxed, see if you can daydream about having a similar pleasurable experience in the future one year, three years or five years down the road…

-What does this feel like in your body…

-Could you feel this way all the time…

-Take time to become familiar with the feel of this changed space in your body so that you can come back to it in the future…

-Can you celebrate the sensual pleasure of this body felt sensation…

-Can you give thanks for the safe place you have created and the unlimited opportunity for pleasure that you have been blessed with…

-Remind yourself of how quickly time flies…

-Can you practice living one day at a time -- making each day the best…

-Can you savor this feeling in your body…

-Take time to become familiar with the feel of this changed space in your body so that you can come back to it in the future…

--And realize that you can always come back…

-And that you will always be welcome here…

-And when you're ready, you can gently bring your attention back to the outer world…

-But you can take with you to the outer world your body felt sense of peace and calm that is available to you in this special place inside you…

-And as you return to the outer world, give thanks for this ability to go inside…

End of "Optimistic Future Visualization"

Notes:

Protocol Script 5:
"Increasing Confidence – Kicking It Up a Notch

"Increasing Confidence - Kicking It Up a Notch"

-Let yourself relax in a safe comfortable spot...

-It is okay if you are sitting, or if you are lying down...

-So long as you are comfortable and relaxed...

-Now focus your attention on your breathing...

-Take a deep breath and notice fresh oxygen entering your body...

-and when you exhale, feel the release of tension and stress...

-and as you are focusing on your breathing --

-notice how your abdomen rises and falls with each breath...

-Just breathe in calmness and relaxation...

-while you exhale tension and stress...

-and if other thoughts crowd your mind that is okay...

-just gently turn your focus back to your breathing...

-and breathe in calmness and relaxation...

-while you exhale tension and stress...

-When you are ready, picture yourself somewhere that is safe and beautiful...

-It can be a place where you have experienced contentment and joy in the past --

-or it can be a place that you make up in your imagination...

-Just let yourself daydream that you are in this safe and beautiful place...

-Notice how comfortable your body feels in this special place...

-Notice any pleasing aromas, sights, or sounds...

-How do these pleasing aromas, sights or sounds make you feel in your body...

-Is there music playing...

-Is the sun shining in your special place...

-Is it daytime or nighttime?

-Is anybody there with you in your special place?

-Notice how happy and relaxed you are in this safe and beautiful place...

-Notice the calmness and relaxation in your body

-and if other thoughts crowd your mind that is okay...

-just gently turn your focus back to your breathing

-and with each breath, inhale calmness and relaxation

-and exhale tension and stress

-Take some time to enjoy and explore this safe and beautiful spot

-Breath in calmness and relaxation --

-and exhale tension and stress

-Notice how this calmness and relaxation feels in your body

-Let go of whatever may be bothering you in the moment

-Just release the tension and stress

-and welcome the calmness and relaxation

-Give thanks for this special place where you can relax and be safe

-and realize that you can always return to this special place

-Whenever you want, you can experience this peace and relaxation

-Now savor this feeling in your body

-Take time to notice how your body feels in this safe place

-and realize that you can always come back --

-You will always be welcome here

End of Relaxation Material

Continue with "Increasing Confidence – Kicking It Up a Notch"

-Recall your daydream where you pictured your future life with more special, pleasurable experiences like the ones you have savored in the past...

-And if one pleasant experience stands out, then see if you can locate where you experience this pleasant sensation in your body...

-And just relax, enjoy, and savor this experience as much as you like...

-And notice, as much is possible, where you are, what you are doing and who is around you...

-And, without stressing or straining, see if you can locate in your body where this pleasant feeling is located...

-Can you picture this delightful feeling seeping into every cell in your body...?

-Imagine that this wonderful feeling projects a soft, warm, invisible light all around you...

-And that, although other people cannot see this light, they can feel its pleasant aura...

-And, being in your safe place, comfortable and relaxed, see if you can daydream about having a similar pleasurable experience in the future one year, three years, or five years down the road...

-Take some time to notice the details of what this feels like in your body...

-Notice if you can identify a feeling of confidence that you can feel this way all the time...

-Where is that feeling located in your body... Is it stronger in any one particular area... Where is it centered...

-As you are enjoying this body felt sensation, can you picture what your posture is like, how you are standing in this special place...

-What expression is on your face, are you smiling, are you speaking, what does this feel like in your face...

-If you are speaking, how does your voice sound... Is it soft, or strong, are you laughing...

-And notice that you are breathing in calmness and exhaling tension...

-And how relaxed and comfortable you are in this safe place...

-Can you dial up the body felt sensation of your sense of confidence in the future...

-Can you imagine that there is a knob or dial on each cell that allows you to increase the quantity of your body felt sensation...

-Take time to see if you can kick this whole thing up a notch...

-While you are comfortable and relaxed, notice that your delightful body felt sensation is overflowing and radiating outward from your body and energizing anyone that may be around you...

-What does this feel like in your body...

-Could you feel this way all the time...

-Take time to become familiar with the feel of this changed space in your body so that you can come back to it in the future...

-Can you celebrate the sensual pleasure of this body felt sensation...

-Can you give thanks for the safe place you have created and the unlimited opportunity for pleasure that you have been blessed with...

-Can you give thanks for the time you have left in this life...

-Can you practice living one day at a time -- making each day the best...

-Can you savor this feeling in your body...

-Take time to become familiar with the feel of this changed space in your body, so that you can come back to it in the future...

-And realize that you can always come back...

-And that you will always be welcome here…

-And when you're ready, you can gently bring your attention back to the outer world…

-But you can take with you to the outer world your body felt sense of peace and calm that is available to you in this special place inside you…

-And as you return to the outer world, give thanks for this ability to go inside…

    End of "Increasing Confidence – Kicking It Up a Notch"

Notes:

Appendix B
Making Your Own Script Recordings

Now that you've read Cancer as an Opportunity, and you want to try making your own recordings - great!! What follows are some points to keep in mind and ideas to stoke the fires of your own creativity.

Ways to Record

Most computers, smart phones and tablets have a built in, easy-to-use, record function. Perhaps the easiest way to start out is to play your favorite music in the background and start reading one of the book's scripts or your own version. Voila! Your own inspirational recording custom-made for you, by you.

If you are inclined to get a little fancier, there are programs available either as free downloads or as software for purchase that act as a sound studio with the capability to record, add background tracks, adjust sound levels, add special effects, convert sound file types, etc.

In the freeware realm, a good program is Audacity – open source, surprisingly sophisticated for being free, and highly rated. Here's the web site link: http://www.audacityteam.org/. The user manual and help topics can be downloaded from the same site.

There are many audio recording/mixing software programs available for purchase. Generally, these programs range anywhere from $40 to $100 depending on the capabilities you need and how many bells and whistles you want. If you have never worked with audio software before, you might want to download a free program first, play with it, and see if you find it helpful. Maybe a simple recording on a phone or tablet is all you need.

This appendix won't go into the specific steps of how to use a particular sound program as the "click here, click there" will be a little bit different depending on the program and will be covered in that program's user manual.

Background Music

This can be as simple as recording your favorite song or album selection playing in the background to buying specialized music and mixing two or more sound tracks together using a sound program. The nice thing is that you can start simple (and free), and later move up to involved (and not-so-free). A good source for unique background music is enlightenedaudio.com. Although the full version of a piece must be purchased, you can try a brief clip at no cost.

Nature sounds – waves, crackling fire, rain, night sounds - are also effective backgrounds. Generally, this type of background effect must be purchased, but it isn't overly expensive. Alternatively, there are apps available that have electronic "nature" reproductions which frequently are free and sound very life-like. Check the free Apps store on your smart phone or tablet and look under sleep or meditation themes.

YouTube is another source for ideas and, in some cases, music or sound clips. Frequently, people with similar interests in relaxation or meditation will put a link on their videos to purchase their recordings.

Appendix C

Contact Information for the Author

Thomas Myers

CancerAsAnOpportunity@gmail.com

Websites

cancerasanopportunity.com

tamcoforensic.com

chinatradeinstitute.com

www.ingramcontent.com/pod-product-compliance
Lightning Source LLC
Chambersburg PA
CBHW071306110426
42743CB00042B/1191